Patterns in the Chaos

Reflections in Sawdust

by David Scott-Morgan

© Lifeware Publishing
www.lifewarepublishing.com
First Published January 2012

Patterns in the Chaos
Edition 2
October 2014

Edited by Mandy Scott-Morgan

Cover art by Stephanie Sungbin Huh

ISBN 978-1-291-37466-7

The right of David Scott-Morgan to
be identified as the author of this work
has been asserted by him in accordance with
the Copyright, Designs and Patents Act 1988.

A note from the author

This book is not meant to be an academic work of facts and figures; it represents my recollections from times past and items culled from diaries and scribblings. I know that over time, stories are fixed in a mythical script and happenings fade from the mind but these are my stories – not mythical at all, but only as true as I can recall them!

This second edition has been produced on the wings of new web-based 'self-publishing' technology. Wonderful as this is, if you are looking at the hard copy version, I must apologise for the sorry rendition of photographs. It simply is not possible to get them better (of course the electronic version is not affected by this limitation). Despite everything, for me, getting 'Patterns' this far is a real victory!

I'd be delighted to hear from you if you have any comments: dave@lifewarepublishing.com

David Scott-Morgan

In memory of absent friends:

Paul Goodall
John 'Upsy' Downing
John 'Pank' Panteney
Frank Skarth Haley
Warren 'The Bird' Samet
Carl 'Charlie' Wayne
Pete Oliver
Kevin 'Kex' Gorin
Kelly Groucutt
Jim Cleary
Ralph Hitchcock

CONTENTS

	Introduction	3
1	EARLY DAYS	5
2	ALF, UNCLE JOE & ELO!	21
3	BIRMINGHAM BLUES	31
4	SEVENTIES	63
5	THE TIME TOUR	91
6	ALL YOU NEED IS CASH!	109
7	FLYING	137
8	ALCHEMY	157
9	ROMANIA	165
10	METAMORPHOSIS	177
11	HINDSIGHT	197
	Epilogue	209
	Discography	212

Unless otherwise noted, all photographs are copyright David Scott-Morgan.
Please do not reproduce any of these without permission.

Preface

People ask me: "You used to be Dave Morgan, now you are David Scott-Morgan. How come?"

Yes I used to be Dave Morgan. But everything changed for me in just one day. On April 10 1996. The day before that Mandy and I were not an item and from that day on, we have not stopped being an item. For most people that would not warrant any belief in divine intervention but in my case, I knew it then and I know it now – Mandy and I being together is nothing short of miraculous.

I wanted to announce that to everyone so I pinched a bit of Mandy's name and became David Scott-Morgan.

Now as I write, we have been together sixteen years and I feel that my book 'Patterns in the Chaos' should be about the time leading up to Mandy and I getting together. What has happened subsequent to that is so very different to what went before.

Yes, I changed my name and Mandy and I were married in April 1997. We had not been married many months when the phone rang: It was the pastor of the little church in Tile Cross, the one just down the road from where I had lived back in the *Early Days,* the same church, albeit under another name and another pastor, where years ago my mother had married Alf.

"Could I come to his church and do a concert next May?" he asked.

"Tell him yes," said Mandy, as if we were hoofing before the footlights every night of the week. I dutifully said, "Yes" with all the conviction of a man who means "No," and then after hanging up, asked Mandy:

"How on earth are we going to do a concert?"

"We can play some music and in between the songs you can tell them your story" she said.

"I have a story?"

"Yes!"

So I do…

INTRODUCTION

I've heard it said that an average reading rate is three words per second. Three *things* per second is easy for me to remember because I happen to know that an aeroplane turns very nicely at three *degrees* per second. At that rate it takes just two minutes to do a complete twizzle – that is, one orbit. And two minutes – I am told – are exactly how long this 'blurb' should take to read. Any longer and I'm in trouble. So I'll stop wasting time?!…

The Lord Mayor and Lady Mayoress were at an Indian restaurant, the one that we frequent a mile or so from where we live. It was a special presentation and the restaurant owner had invited along Mandy and I, and my friend Karl, to meet with these dignitaries:

"We are not worthy!" Karl said with a gentle stoop of mock bowing and we all laughed – the Lord Mayor too. We chatted in the aisle between the tables while to one side, the Lady Mayoress was firmly ensconced at a table and engrossed in conversation with the woman seated opposite. Meanwhile her husband was on an invisible elastic lanyard, prodigiously navigating the chairs and tables to say *hello,* shake hands and then be catapulted back to our scrum position between the tables. All the time, cameras flashed and the restaurant owner strutted past beaming with pride.

"How do you like the job?" I asked, unable to avert my gaze completely off his broad chest, bedecked with shiny dangling things. "Oh it's great fun" he said with a faint swagger and big impish smile as if being the Lord Mayor was a schoolboy prank.

Yes I can see how being the Lord Mayor is fun. There are many jobs that can only ever really be described as 'fun'. I can understand his response because I remember that being with a famous group was hard work – pressured, gruelling – but I never think of that; I just ponder on what immense, incredible fun it all was. What a gift it is to play with a great rock 'n' roll group – or to be Lord Mayor for that matter!

Now I think it only right that I explain how I came to be in bands, and a famous one at that. So that means going right back to the year zero and the rickety dark streets of post war Birmingham, where I hailed from, wide eyed with wonder at the world we found ourselves in. A world full of giants. Of Churchill and Stalin. Of Chaplin, Brando, Elvis and then – the Beatles.

Yes, Einstein may have unlocked the secret to the atom but the Beatles unlocked the door to all our unspoken and undreamed aspirations. The Beatles changed our world and now we can look back and see it in a different light, but then… we were caught up in a tide of history that swept all before it. The fab four distilled a potion so strong everybody wanted a slug of it. It was a tonic of joy and cheek, the most essential ingredients of good music.

No, I never made a career decision to be a musician; I don't think many of us did. In my case the decisions were always in the negative: not to work anymore in the factory fettering bicycle frames with a file from eight thirty to five; or in the scrap metal yard with a spanner and a pair of pliers, ripping apart discarded motor-bikes and other mechanical implements. Music was always an escape from all that but never a strategy worth banking on or planning for. The bottom line was, I never thought I was good enough to be 'anyone' in music or anything else, and this vortex of mental hari-kari would have become a self-fulfilling prophecy were it not for the intervention of a benevolent time and fortune and, of course the great pattern-maker, my secret benefactor.

So I guess in putting together this book I have been trying to squeeze out of the twists and turns of my journey any and every bit of fun that I could find lurking there. For fun, laughter and the joy of being there are the things that ricochet through life and never lose their healing power from being remembered again.

I have to admit though, that in all of this I did very little planning or scheming. I did not so much aim myself as find myself being drawn up in a giant vacuum cleaner to be set down in places I did not ask to be – often didn't even want to be. Nevertheless, there I was! Sometimes it seemed that I was just totally in the wrong place and the wrong time, but actually I never was. I can see that now and so I called this book 'Patterns in the Chaos' – The chaos is all mine and the patterns are all divine.

ONE – EARLY DAYS

According to the grown-ups, I was a sickly child. Apparently I spent some months in an isolation hospital with suspected whooping cough. I have no recollection of it, only the interminable visits to doctors, and my frail physical frame being dragged into parked black vans labelled 'National Radiological Unit' – the mobile government torture chambers housing cold X-ray machines.

It was post-war Birmingham and compared with today, most of us were undernourished, dishevelled and slightly ailing in some manner. But in one respect, my family were better off than most – we were one of the only households in our road with transport. Dad had a job as travelling projectionist with the European Economic League and had the use of the company van.

One of my earliest memories is of being in the back of that little Austin Seven van... Suddenly the van swerves:

"Oh No," says dad.

Mom screams: "What's the matter?"

"We're stuck in the tram lines," he gasps.

I look out of the window. Yes, the narrow wheels are in line with the tram tracks

Mom squeals again. It wasn't unusual to hear mom shriek especially whilst being driven along the 'horse road' as she called it. She had a nervous, fearful disposition and dad knew how to gain maximum prank benefit out of it. Up ahead I can see the tramlines divide from one line into two. We swerve comically again along one of the lines, just like the Keystone Cops did in the silent black and white movies that dad would show in the living room at weekends.

"Raymond, do something!"

"I can't, we're stuck. We'll have to wait until we get to the terminus," he says with a chuckle and a glint in his eye.

"It's no laughing matter," she says sternly but dad just laughs.

We travelled down the Pershore Road like that until the inevitable tram appeared in the distance ahead and slowly loomed larger and larger – along with the volume of mom's pleas, until finally, dad got off the lines! It's hard to imagine now but there was a time when people believed that car wheels could actually get stuck in tram lines!

It was just the same at the seaside. Dad would creep the van ever closer to the cliff edge, claiming trouble with the gears or the brakes, while the small compartment would be filled with mom's screaming interspersed with loud guffaws from dad. As always I sat in the back, a bemused spectator.

My young life was filled with laughter – a side effect of my godly upbringing. Mom and dad were real Christians – the front door was always open to anybody in trouble, and hymns were sung at full throttle on Sundays! Dad would play an old pedal organ – (ah, that old organ – how I remember its entrance in to our world: with me sat on top, it was transported on a cart pulled by dad and granddad three miles from the leafy suburb of Kingstanding to the big Georgian terraces of inner city Aston). It was worth their effort: that pedal organ was to be the focus of much of the entertainment at our home. Dad played it while he and mom and whoever else was present, would brim the room full of singing. He had never been taught to read music, he just played by ear. When we moved from the high ceilinged rooms at Aston to the house on the brand new council estate at Tile Cross, that old organ moved with us.

Dancing Girls

Dad came home late one night to be greeted by an indignant mom wanting to know where he had been.

"Ssshhhh" he said, with a finger to his lips and a smirk on his face, "they'll hear you."

"They? – WHO?" demanded mom, "I hope you haven't brought anyone here at this time of night Raymond."

"Yes I have," whispered dad, "they're just outside."

"What! Oh I do think that's too bad," mom gasped in her tone of ultimate displeasure.

"I've bought a couple of dancing girls home for you Clara."

Clara was dad's nickname for Mom. It was more of a private taunt, that name with its hard sound often teamed up alongside mention of 'Carayilie Street,' a Hockley slum area where Vinnie grew up as a girl. Mom had no similar ridicule to heap upon dad for the Welsh mining community of Risca, from where dad had migrated to Birmingham in search of work before the war.

"You've done WHAT!," she exploded. "Dancing Girls? – Well you can just take them out again and go right back out with them. You're not coming in here with any fancy pieces and that's a fact. You mark my words, they are not welcome here and neither are you if that's your gallop. So there!"

"I'll just go and get them," said dad ignoring her and disappearing into the hall.

Dad came back reaching into a paper bag: "here they are" he said as he carefully pulled out two hand-carved, decorously painted sheet wood reliefs… Ladies in full swing with their skirts flowing against an imaginary wind as they twirled around.

The reason I can remember this story so well is because I heard it recounted so many times whenever a visitor to the house would remark about the dancing ladies hanging on the wall

Yes those dancing girls lived on our wall and were to outlast dad, dancing for another twenty years after he had gone and never growing a day older. There above the pedal organ, they would attract the attention of the many visitors we had – the bread man, the milkman, the postman, the insurance man, the doctor, the vicar, and of course the omnipresent neighbour – as they sat sipping tea around the living room table. Mom would tell each how those girls came into the house late one night and how she almost threw them and dad out before he had the chance to get to the punch line.

As well as these pranks I recall that dad always seemed to be involved in the wackiest of enterprises. On the occasion of the Queen's Coronation in 1953, he erected a giant marquee in the front garden. Bunting, cakes and chairs were provided by all the neighbours and on the joyous day, everybody in the street was revelling at our house, number 17. I was enlisted to help stoke the merriment by being pressed into what you might call my show biz debut. Dad set up a raised wooden plank *stage* and coaxed me in front of a bright light to mime an Al Jolson song. From this tiny platform inside the marquee I remember I was shrivelled in embarrassment at the ordeal of singing, or pretending to, in front the white light, behind which sat that terrifying audience.

A year later, in 1954, at Haringay Arena in London, I remember Mom and Dad pushing me forward again, this time to join the multitude of people responding to Billy Grahams' appeal to "Come forward for salvation".

"Go on David" they said, nudging me to join the crowd moving forward across the football pitch to give their lives to Jesus. And there I was, wanting to go and not wanting to go, all at the same time paralysed with excruciating embarrassment at twelve years old even!

"Go on" they said again, and somewhat grudgingly, go I did. Maybe they understood something about the importance of being there, of just turning up even when your heart isn't in it.

But life for me took a dramatic turn when I was thirteen – dad died suddenly leaving me alone with mom. From there, any belief I had in God evaporated, and relations with mom went steadily downhill.

Dad dying just messed everything up. I was at Bordesley Green Technical School, a sort of downsized Grammar School. I can't remember quite how or why but I went from being at nearly top of the class to the very bottom after dad died. It was probably something to do with the way it happened.

It was 1956, the year Britain went to war over the Suez Canal, but all I knew was that dad had been feeling unwell for several days. He needed some medicine. So, late one night, we drove together in his van to the only place open, Boots the Chemist, in the city centre. We had parked up and were walking along the streets when dad bent down to pick up a scrap of paper... He stood motionless for a moment looking at it. I peered over his shoulder – or I think it was more under his shoulder – to see for myself. It said simply: 'Prepare to meet thy God'. Nothing else – Just like on those sandwich boards that men used to carry around in that era.

Two days later, he died. He was 42, a guy brimming with humour and practical jokes, in the prime of life. Mom was devastated. I was numb. I didn't cry, or rather I didn't cry in front of anyone else.

Later, after the funeral, I was in the house with mom – she was upstairs in the bedroom. Suddenly there was a shriek like I had never heard. I rushed upstairs to find her just standing there, wailing.

"What's wrong mom?"

She didn't answer, just sobbed. On the bed lay dad's clothes. She had been going through the paraphernalia in his pockets.

"Mom, what's wrong?"

She croaked something and lifted a hand to show me a piece of paper. I recognised it immediately and said shakily: "Dad found that on New Street the night we went to get the medicine."

Nothing more was spoken about it, but as I recall now, and as I have many times realised, that scrap of paper seemed to carry upon it the most awful message, the most dreadful truth she could ever have received: Her God, who she loved dearly, had taken her man, who she loved dearly!

Nothing could have tested her faith more. I remember well the scoffing about God she had to endure from relatives, but she never lost her faith. Unlike me. Whatever grudging regard I had for mom's *godliness* disappeared rapidly.

It was all too much for me. I believed God had done it, but that only made it worse. It was impossible to make any sense of it. I just went to ground. Somewhere I thought: 'if I keep my head down, maybe He won't notice me!' – Surely, God must be someone who zaps his pals for no reason.

It was a whole lifetime later, in June 1988, that I laid myself down before God in awe of His goodness and soon after that, mom and I began gradually to become friends, because we never really were – throughout all that time!

But I am getting ahead of myself…

Bikes

It was the sixties, an era when a policeman would stop a speeding car by stepping out into the road and putting his hand up. That was all it took. To ignore the command of a policeman was, to all intents and purposes, unthinkable. Today of course, when roads are crammed full of traffic and the authority of the law of the land open to question, the result would be one seriously flattened copper, but back then, not to stop was really not an option worth considering.

Order flowed from an unspoken, abiding regard for the *powers that be*, and was maintained within clear boundaries. What lay beyond those boundaries was largely unknown.

Constable Ferris was a man used to stepping out in front of speeding vehicles, to be precise, speeding motor bikes and scooters. He had also learned to be adept at skipping backwards, as sometimes the invitation to stop for a chat was beyond the capability of our feeble brakes. Yet despite all the provocations, Constable Ferris maintained an air of amiable, authoritative familiarity with us as he policed the quiet suburb of Marston Green. It was a patch devoid of rebellion were it not for the fact that we imported it nightly from nearby Tile Cross. A race from the chip shop at Marston Green to the bus terminus at Tile Cross was virtually mandatory for the 'gang' of which I was a member, some say a ring-leader.

The best of us, or the worst – depending on which way you looked at it, was Paul Goodall. Nobody could beat Paul. I should know, I tried often enough. I could never beat him although I drove as if without attachment to this mortal coil. I learned that the secret to winning was really to convince your opponent that you were absolutely stark raving mad, and that required demonstrations of maximum lunacy. Really, you could always depend on someone else's sanity giving you a tyre's width of lead, if you could make them believe you were mad enough to kill both of you otherwise.

Although I could beat most anybody else in a race, I could never beat Paul, and never did, not once. Paul *was* completely mad, whereas the rest of us were merely of dubious sanity. I thought the world of him, enough to loan him my scooter, which he promptly crashed.

I saw him do so many crazy things to be first in a race, or just to cause consternation, and sometimes he would pull a stunt for no reason at all, just because! –

There were four or five of us, biking down a grass track in Chelmsley Woods – not racing, just ambling along. Paul came past me and then, when he was just ahead, he turned around to look at me while a silly grin broke out all over his face. He just sat there, staring square at me, with one outstretched hand gripping the empty pillion seat behind him. We went along like that, Paul not looking where he was going. Up ahead a T-junction loomed with a nasty prickly hedge beyond and I started to shout and point to him… but he never batted an eyelid. He sat there looking back at me until he and his bike collided with the barrier of bushes, branches and nettles. He went through it to the field beyond while his bike was impaled sideways on the thicket. We pulled him back through the hole he'd punched. He was sporting cuts and bruises, and still wearing that silly grin. He knew all along that the hedge was there, he did it just for a laugh!

One time I remember we were both up together *before the beak* (I can't remember what for). We were standing side by side right in front of the bench. The proceedings were at that point where they are about to pass sentence and the magistrate leaned over and said:

"Are there any previous convictions?"

The voice of a clerk came from behind us:

"Yes your honour, for Mr. Morgan there is …. blah blah blah..," – an enormous catalogue of embarrassing infractions – speeding, driving without lights, without care, without a licence…

I stood there listening to this litany of disgrace and the only ray of sunshine in my mind was the thought of Paul's record, and how that at least, would put mine into the shade, but big time.

The Clerk droned on to the end of my list, shuffled some papers and then said:

"And for Mr.Goodall, no previous convictions your honour!"

I gasped and looked around at Paul. But he just stood grinning in his mischievous way. They had lost all his records but remembered all mine!

Then one night Paul appeared on my doorstep looking very bedraggled and shivering with cold:

"Can I come in?" he whimpered.

"Yes of course, what's up?"

"I'm freezing" he said. He didn't have his bike – he'd been disqualified from driving.

"What on earth have you been doing to get so cold?"

"I've been lying on the railway line up by Marston Green."

"What?"

Mom brought us both a cup of tea.

He lowered his voice so that she couldn't hear and went on to tell me how he'd decided to end it all. "I'd been lying on the tracks for nearly an hour wondering why no trains were coming down the main London to Birmingham line, and then I remembered – It's the day of the National rail strike!"

He smiled that mischievous grin of his telling me about this and I honestly wasn't sure if the whole thing was just a big practical joke. I didn't really take him seriously.

But a short while later, on 7 March 1962, Paul Goodall gassed himself. They found him in his parent's front room. A note said it was because a girl had finished with him. The route out of town to the big A47 trunk road led past Paul's house. I can't remember where we were going that day, just the commotion outside his house making us stop and ask someone: "What's happened?"

Paul's funeral was the first I ever recall going to (I didn't go to dad's, I couldn't face it). There were eight car-loads of mourners plying a snail's-pace to the short service at Yardley Crematorium. Paul's coffin rode up front in a grey Daimler and I couldn't help but think he would have been insulted by the speed. It hit me hard, him dying like that. I felt as if death had come to spar with me again, and leave me once more, punch-drunk with the pointlessness of it all. Paul had been indestructible. In another epoch he might have won medals for some audacious dash before a machine-gun nest. But in this epoch – my epoch, his jovial nonchalance for all things mortal was sealed forever in that wooden box placed squarely in front of us that day.

Somebody said how it was losing his licence that had taken away his reason for living. It was true, Paul lived for kicks and the thrill of doing battle with the moving scissors of vehicles and obstacles. Yet it was none of those deadly foes that brought him down, but a girl he barely knew. Her and the devil of rejection.

Girls & Groups

Yes, girls had appeared into our teenage concerns and where once the talk would be about the many crashes we had, soon it gravitated to include the opposite sex. For me, bikes and girls slowly cross-faded to become groups and girls.

It was 1961, the year Yuri Gagarin became the world's first spaceman. A friend named Roger bought a guitar, and so I bought a guitar too. It was so difficult to play, I almost gave up. Then I saw a book in a shop: 'Play in a Day' it announced on the cover. Bert Weedon sold millions of copies of that little book to people like me.

It had diagrams of a guitar fret-board with numbered dots showing which finger to put onto which string. Of course it should have been titled 'Play in a Lifetime,'… but never mind, it was a great help. Yet despite all this good assistance it still took me ages before I was able to change chords fast enough to play a song.

The cross-over to music took awhile, but finally became complete for me one frosty night in January 1963. We were all sat around the Formica-covered table at a city centre café, sipping cups of tea while our bikes were parked up outside. Suddenly the juke box exploded into my reality with a sound like I had never heard: It was the Beatles singing 'Please Please Me'. The chords at the end went round and around in my head, I was entranced. I thought it was beautiful. The brute magic of it captured me as it did most everybody else.

A pal named Mick Andrews sang with a group that rehearsed at St Peters church in Tile Cross and soon he pressed me into service on rhythm guitar. We fumbled around in varying degrees of ineptitude as 'The Moonrakers' and then metamorphosed into 'The Jaguars' before disappearing altogether. It was shortly afterwards that I joined a proper group – one that actually got paid to play!

At last, the big time! It was July 1963 and I was one of Jeff Silvas's 'Four Strangers'. but there was one slight problem – I couldn't really play! I had real difficulty keeping time. My left hand was okay at chords, but my right hand was lousy at rhythm, no more that a stuttering sail jerking in approximation to the beat. To compound matters, I found it impossible to play with a plectrum, and resorted to strumming with my fingers so as to avoid the embarrassment of having my pick zoom across the dance-hall, catapulted by my strings with a strident, heralding twang.

All of this I tried to keep secret of course, while I watched other musicians with envy and shame. I was the 'rhythm' guitarist, and this gross misrepresentation of fact went largely un-reported. All the same, I felt a fraud. I thought *someone is sure to notice I'm not really very good at this!*

(Even now, Mandy and I have a standing joke that my strumming should carry a health warning – if anyone is dancing to it, they are in danger of dislocating something if I miss a beat! However, now I have long lost any insecurity about being a musician, I know that music is something inside that just finds the best way it can of getting out.)

I resolved to do what I could, and soon discovered that one thing I could do was write songs. Chords really interested me and the Beatles were putting them together in novel, exciting ways.

One day I came upon a new collection of chords myself. I hummed a tune around them, made up some sickly embarrassing words – and *hey presto*, I had written a song! It was called 'I do'. I didn't really think it was any good, but other people picked up on it. I was encouraged and wrote more, and tried not to worry too much about my faltering guitar style.

Obviously it wasn't a proper job. It couldn't possibly last. Everybody said so – it must be true. Surely before too long I would have to knuckle down and become a responsible member of the great multitude of they whose lives beat with as much thrill as a metronome, but who cares? For now I could get a girl to go out with me because I played music in a group. I didn't have to 'dance' and do all that silly gyrating around on the floor – all that pruning and poncing stuff around the edges of the dance area.

I had discovered a vital truth – I could prune and ponce standing bolt upright, providing I was on a stage holding a guitar, and I'd be just as desirable to the girls as all those swaggering types down below.

Academy

Then one day our singer – Jeff Silvas – left the group and we contemplated how to carry on without him as 'The Strangers'. Bill Miller, the lead guitarist, took over most of the singing, but looked to me to get stuck in too. The call to stand in front of a microphone and warble was a challenge I both feared and prized at the same time. So I practised for hours while I was on my own – driving. Inside the echo-ey cab of my van, I would sing songs over and over until I had honed enough of the squeaks and rattles out of my flimsy resonations to dare bring them before somebody else. Even then, when I got in front of the microphone, it often sounded dreadful, and I had to go back to the rehearsal room behind the steering wheel of my van…

I spent a long time in the cab of that van – I used to date a girl who lived in the countryside, south of Stratford-upon-Avon, and it took about an hour to drive there. That was two hours of singing practise per night. It was in that cab, bellowing out over the racket of the engine, that I discovered the techniques I needed in order to conceal the fact I had no inbred singing ability. I knew that whatever I was to acquire had to be imparted by method, not nature.

You have to understand that being in a group at that time was really about learning how to mimic – My hero was John Lennon and I practised until I could impersonate his style of singing to a tee. Not anyone's tee, just my tee. I got immense pleasure from rasping out his lines to myself.

Along with singing, I would practise 'speaking' – yes speaking. Something had made me aware of how bad my speech was – maybe it was being around my girl friend's family, with their slightly Shakespearean country English. Maybe it was serving afternoon teas to the toffs who stopped at the impromptu café they ran in the garden of their farmhouse. But somewhere along the line it dawned on me that the slovenly Brummie dialect I had harvested from birth needed a translator to be understood anywhere outside of a Birmingham factory or pub.

There was a feeling amongst my workmates down at Colmore Depot motor stores that you were a traitor to your class if you spoke anything approaching the Queen's English, but I came to the conclusion that good speech had to do simply with how well you wanted other people to understand what you were trying to say. So little by little, I tried to improve the way I spoke, ignoring the jibes of workmates and peers who would label anyone pretending to correct pronunciation as a 'ponce'.

Yes I ran my own academy of elocution and singing lessons in that Morris J2 van. I was my own instructor, my own audience. I booed or cheered, I organised the lessons, I set the exams and I marked the papers.

I was a 'Stranger' on rhythm guitar for a total of two years before the reality of my paltry guitar skills got the better of me. It seemed no amount of practice could turn me into a proper musician. I left the group and made a decision: I would become a proper storeman for the Colmore Depot company instead. At least that was something attainable. I still played with a group and wrote some songs, but it ceased to be a priority.

I started to turn up on time for work, a miracle that did not go un-noticed. Then I began redesigning the stores filing system, and organising the racks carrying the spare parts. I was doing really well at it, the management were humming my praises, right up until one day in January 1966. A call came through for me on the little sales office telephone:

"Who?"

"My name is Danny King" the voice repeated.

"Oh hello, yes, of course I've heard of you"

"And you are the Dave Morgan who wrote this song – the one called 'It's an ill wind that blows'?"

"Er yes I am. How did you get to hear that?"

"I have just been listening to a tape of it down at Johnny Hayne's studio and I want to tell you: I don't care if you're short, ugly, bald or covered in spots – I want you in my group! Come down the Cedar Club tonight and we'll talk some more about it, okay?"

"Oh, er thanks, yeah, right… Okay then, I'll see yer at the Cedar tonight."

That was the end of my career in the stores of Colmore Depot. I lost the job for consistently turning up late after joining Danny King's 'Mayfair Set'.

Dad working his projector at a work's canteen film show circa 1950.

Tile Cross

Tile Cross was the name of the new estate built in the early 50's on green fields to the east of Birmingham - It featured six-storey and three-story flats along with terraced houses made of concrete, like ours shown here. The estate was part of Birmingham's post-war slum-clearance project. Here mom is on the doorstep of our house in Briddsland Road, Tile Cross (wherever did the name 'Briddsland' come from?? The mind boggles when speculating how the chaps in Birmingham City Council invented names for their roads).

Above: a new bike for me.
Below: a woman's work is never done... Mom in the kitchen

My Mini-Cooper on the drive at Tile Cross.

Mom and Joe at Brill, Buckinghamshire.

TWO – ALF, UNCLE JOE & ELO!

Alf

One day mom dropped a bombshell on me: She was considering getting married again!

Alf Print had been her friend since before the war, even before she met Raymond. He had come from a fairly well to do family who, for reasons I never did quite fathom, had disowned and disinherited him as a young man. By 1962 he was down on his luck and living at the Salvation Army Hostel in the centre of Birmingham, a residency that always seemed to be on the verge of summary termination: I remember one occasion when mom interceded on his behalf to keep them from throwing him out. Alf was one of the people in mom's orbit of care but when she announced that she intended to marry him I felt as if that old steamroller was revving up again to roll over me and do me in. Mom seemed convinced that it was God's will for her to marry Alf. I was horrified and indignant.

"Does that mean my name will change to David Print?" I barked at her.

She didn't know the answer. Enquiries were made into protocol and legalities and it transpired that I would remain a Morgan. It was just as well. That would probably have been the very last straw.

But all the objections of her family, and all my protestations, came to nought, and in the summer of 1962 mom became Mrs. Print at the little church up the road from our home where she went to worship every Sunday.

Three months after mom married Alf, the Cuban missile crisis flared up and for a while I existed like everyone else, as a zombie going through the motions – get up, catch a bus, go to work, come home, all the while expecting the enormous bang that would announce the end of the world. Then as quick as it had flared up it was gone. I was at work at Colmore Depot, on tenterhooks, wondering what would happen when the Americans intercepted the Soviet ships in the Atlantic. Suddenly someone was running around shouting: "It's over – the Russian ships have turned around! They're going back home. Khrushchev's backed down!"

During this time Mom's brother Joe also came to live with us in our council house at Tile Cross. Uncle Joe was a fugitive from other relatives who had tired of him.

Both Alf and Joe suffered with their 'nerves' as mom called it – a euphemism for 'mental health problems', itself a sop to political correctness that belies stark reality like disinfectant masks the smell of a drain. Whereas Joe's affliction would manifest as inertia and depression, Alf's would surface in fits of violent rage. Then at other times, he would have the temperament and disposition of an inoffensive child. You never quite knew what could cause a flare-up, but often it was directed at Mom. He would pass through the house like an enraged bull destroying things, often things of special significance like dad's photographs or letters, and afterwards he would cry like a baby for forgiveness.

It was in one of these eruptions that Alf smashed the TV to pieces with an axe. My friend Mick Andrews bought us round a replacement, a second-hand one from the TV shop where he worked. I remember Mick saying to Alf: "You keep smashing them up and I'll keep bringing them. You'll be knee-deep in tellies!"

Then in July 1964, Alf died suddenly, releasing the household from its state of simmering stress and mom from her pledge to God. She had kept Alf off the streets and given him a home. Now all she had to do was look after Joe.

Uncle Joe

Yes my uncle Joe alternated between being the court jester of the house, supplying song, dance and seaside postcard jokes, while other times taking on the attributes of a zombie: silent, unresponsive, shuffling past like one of the undead in a B movie.

Everyone scoffed at Joe, and I was at the front of the queue. Joe was the 'bag man' who would go around picking up waste paper from the street, who would drop everything to help somebody only to be rewarded with insults. He was plagued all his life by mental health problems and disowned by the rest of the family; he was an outcast to all except his sister Vinnie. Nobody wanted Joe around, me included. Mom was his only pal.

Much to my chagrin, Joe lived with us in our two-bed roomed council house in Tile Cross. For years, Joe and I slept in the same bedroom, a grudging arrangement as far as I was concerned. When I complained I was told by mom that Joe "has nowhere else to go, I have to look after him." And that's what she did, she looked after him come hell and high water.

Now it amuses me to recollect the connection that Joe had with a cheeky unassuming teenager who just a few short years later, would climb to the roof of our world and create a music group that became a household name.

I guess it's true that some of you will be reading this because you remember the group ELO – The 'Electric Light Orchestra'. Yes, they were a great group! I got to join them in 1981 and wow, that was a good job to get – especially as I was on the dole at the time!

Jeff

But I'd known Jeff Lynne, the driving force behind ELO, for more than fifteen years before that.

I first bumped into him at a church hall in Shard End, Birmingham in December 1963 – I was playing there with 'Jeff Silvas and the Four Strangers' and he came up in the break to ask if he could "have a go" on my guitar (I don't think he owned one then). I stood watching him strumming the chords to a 'Dave Clark Five' song that was in the charts, never thinking for a moment that this kid would turn out to be a major force in world pop music and have an influence on my life, along with zillions of others, stretching far into the future. At that time, I never even knew his name.

It was more than a year later, in 1965, when I was in 'The Chantelles' that he appeared one day in answer to our advert for a guitarist. I recognised him straight away as the guy who had strummed on my guitar before. Jeff Lynne duly became 'The Chantelles' lead guitarist, a dubious honour seeing as the group was little more than work in progress – I seem to recall we spent more time rehearsing in the drummer's garage than playing gigs. We used to practice – what I thought – rather good three-part harmonies. One time, when we were playing a gig somewhere, I remember singing and thinking 'these harmonies sound a bit sparse', and looking around, saw Jeff stood back from his mic, as if he'd forgotten he was supposed to sing. I caught his eye and motioned for him to join in but he shook his head. I confronted him afterwards but he said,

"I don't want to sing – singing is for wimps! – I just want to play the guitar."

Jeff wouldn't sing with 'The Chantelles' but I knew he *could* sing, and so, much later, it came to pass...

The bass player of 'The Nightriders' called me up one day to ask if I knew of a lead guitarist who could also sing. – I gave him Jeff's number, and then immediately phoned him up to alert him:

"Jeff, I just gave 'The Nightriders' your number cos they're looking for someone to play guitar" ('The Nightriders' were a highly respected local band – Roy Wood had not long left them).

"Oh thanks Dave" Jeff said.

"And Jeff..."

"Yeah?".

"You can sing, right?"

"Yeah," he said catching the hidden message with a muted giggle.

Jeff joined 'The Nightriders', who soon changed their name to 'The Idle Race'.

"'The Idle Race'! – Why do you call yourselves by that silly name?" my mom once asked him.

Jeff fell silent for a second or two, and then said "I can't be bothered to answer that!"

Mom seemed quite convinced we were all wasting our time.

"Time hallows only that which he himself hath made" she would repeat as a dire warning to us all.

Jeff lived about two miles from me – I was on Tile Cross Estate and he was on Shard End Estate – and so we used to pop in on each other, and we were often on the phone when a new 'Beatles' record came out – fawning over it usually. On one occasion I went around to play him a new song I'd just written and we got talking about having a record out – *the ultimate dream*. But in my heart that prospect really belonged in fantasyland, and I said something negative like:

"I don't suppose that anyone out there will ever get to hear my stuff" I remember Jeff shot back immediately with:

"Well they're gonna hear me whether they like it or not!"

How true that statement was. How idle words have the power to condemn, or direct, according to the spirit.

The Move

Then in 1966 a tremor shook the Birmingham music scene, propelled by the vision of local singer Carl Wayne: If you've ever seen the film 'The Dam Busters' you will recall how Squadron Leader Guy Gibson picked out the cream of pilots from all the other RAF squadrons (upsetting quite a few people in the process), in order to create his elite team of airmen. That's what Carl Wayne did – he went around the Birmingham music scene like a head hunter checking off the best talent around, and then made his play. Finally the raid was on and the dam broke – Months of secrecy were ended and Carl unveiled the new super group from Birmingham – 'The Move'.

From Mike Sheridan's 'Nightriders' he took Roy Wood (at the time, Jeff Lynne described Roy as the best guitarist he'd ever seen). From 'The Avengers', he took drummer Bev Bevan, from Danny King's 'Mayfair Set', guitarist Trevor Burton, while from his own band – 'The Vikings', he kept bass-player Ace Kefford. This *Move* reverberated through the Brumbeat groups affecting many others down the line. For some it meant a disastrous loss, while for others, me included, it represented an opportunity to climb another rung up the ladder. The next rung for me was a job with Danny King. For Jeff Lynne it was a job with 'The Nightriders'.

'The Move' were indeed Birmingham's star group and went on to have many hit songs, all written by Roy, but after a few years on the road tensions between them caused first Ace Kefford, and then Trevor Burton to leave. I figured in some of those dramas and I'll speak about that later, but for now let's get back to the ELO family tree: It was during this period that I became friends with Carl Wayne, and Jeff became a pal of Roy Wood.

Jeff came around one day in 1970 clutching a tape he was really excited about. It was a recording he'd made with Roy Wood called '10538 overture' (he'd teamed up with Roy as part of 'The Move' earlier that year). He said that he and Roy were thinking of forming a new group called *the Electric Light Orchestra.*

"The what?" I said, unsure if I'd heard him right or if it was leading up to another one of his jokes.

The convention of group names had already been smashed wide open: 'The Beatles' had led that insurrection. No longer was the star's name followed dutifully two paces behind by the group's name. Identity had become a point of artistic expression in itself, but the name that Jeff had proffered was stretching it a bit in a different direction! An orchestra? Aren't they full of law-abiding musicians who read the dots and wear suits and ties and stuff?

Just about the next thing I heard coming down the grapevine was that 'The Move' had metamorphosed into the new group with that strange name Jeff had told me about, 'The Electric Light Orchestra'. Strangely, Roy left after about six months and everyone expected the Electric Light to switch off fast without his luminance on board, but it didn't. Jeff had bitten hard on the dream, enough to hang on while the setbacks shook him.

While Jeff kept his nose to the grindstone, I bobbed up and down like flotsam on the ebb and flow of fortune. I was in and out of various groups, and in between times in the group known as 'Her Majesty's Social Security' (in case that actually refers to a real act, let me point out that it means I was *on the dole* – collecting welfare from the government).

At one point I was a labourer on a building site but that magically turned into a job playing bass guitar in a night-club residency. That job gave me enough money to take a private pilots licence course but a couple of years later, I was back scraping the barrel of life. In order to keep off the dole, I found myself working for a friend of mine named Steve.

The year was 1976 and Steve was making ornamental brass models of Stevensons' Rocket, which were somewhat strangely in demand. He had a tumble-down workshop in a part of the city that was honeycombed with old Victorian factories, bomb-sites, and slums in the process of being cleared. It was a filthy place with a brick floor and long heavy wooden benches upon which I would fetter and polish brass castings. A radio blared out constantly and one day a song came on that caught my attention immediately –

"That was 'Living Thing' by 'The Electric Light Orchestra'" – the announcer said afterwards.

It made my day. My mate Jeff, on the radio with a great pop song!

I loved it and I knew he'd cracked it. Jeff, with the idea that he and Roy had had of forging a marriage between rock 'n' roll and classical music, had eclipsed the success of all the Birmingham groups before him, and sailed off the edge of our blinkered world, eventually to become a household name in America and beyond. Essentially, like the space station on the cover of his 'Out of the Blue' album, he had escaped the gravity of our petty factional limitations, and was orbiting above, weightlessly unassailable.

For a few years I lost track of Jeff as he toured around. Meanwhile the flotsam rose and fell on the tide, and amazingly, in 1979, I discovered I was the writer of a hit song myself. 'Hiroshima', a song that took me all of fifteen minutes to write in my mom's house ten years before, had become a 'sleeper' hit in Germany, staying in the lower end of the charts for almost a year!

No sooner had I cashed the first cheque than I was off to America. It was in Los Angeles in 1980, as a guest of Richard Tandy that I met up with Jeff again. He had a chalet at a hotel in Beverly Hills and one night we went to the 'club' – I mean THE club, the Polo Lounge – the poshest *do* in town. I remember they wouldn't let Jeff in because he wasn't wearing a jacket.

"We can loan you one sir" the concierge said, and duly rummaged around the cloakroom to emerge with a jacket about twenty sizes too big for him.

"This must've belonged to Orson Welles" Jeff said as we walked in together, giggling. We sat around a table drinking beers and I told him as best I could how good his music had sounded to me from the bottom rung of the ladder, where I'd perchanced to hear it from the working class vista we both knew so well. He was in the middle of recording the music for the film 'Xanadu' at the time, and while I was out there, I got to help out on the demo for the song 'All Over the World'. It was just exhilarating, watching the process of making a record at that level. Jeff and Richard worked so hard at it, going over the song time and again, making small changes, patiently listening for that time when it sits right and doesn't make you lose equilibrium – you know, fall off your stool!

But back home in Birmingham I was astonished by the vibes I picked up from other musicians regarding Jeff's achievements. Many seemed scathing, dismissive or cynical, saying he'd sold out, stolen ideas, was just lucky to be in the right place at the right time, all that kind of stuff. There was one I remember – a drummer, who saw it differently. "Jeff has shown us all the way, he's really done the business, the best of luck to him" he said to me one night in the Elbow Room night club. The others seemed gripped in a 'Conspiracy Theory' mindset that saw everything as the artefact of some alternative reality – where ELO's success had been engineered by big business – or the CIA – or aliens – anyone!

One guitarist got particularly upset when I told him proudly that I'd helped out on Jeff's demo in LA: 'Did he pay you a session fee?' he barked, incensed with the socialist venom of the downtrodden which was the popular mood of the time.

But I'm being unfair. The fact was, I had known Jeff from way back, and I'd heard him say audacious, ridiculous things which later gained the substance of fact. They didn't know that like I did. I knew he had dreamed big and not let go, while others, me included, had dreamed a little and let go a lot.

It was 1981 when Jeff asked me to join his by now, mega-successful group. When I recount to people now just how that came about I often say that he asked me to join and I said 'I'll think about it – and how much are you going to pay me?' to poke fun at the fact I said the quickest 'Yes' possible. The fact is, I was a real fan of Jeff's music – I loved it and felt I understood it. It was hard work rehearsing but it was never hard work supporting Jeff playing that music because it had already built a home in my heart. Playing it was just stoking a fire before a familiar hearth.

The fool on the hill

Now, a song begins as just a little idea. A fragile thing, like a new-born baby. You have to be careful who you show it to, who you allow to hold it – at least until it's grown up some! In the guise of well-wishers, people can speak words over your child which can help propel it toward its destiny or else condemn it to sickness and an early death.

I don't know who Paul McCartney had in mind when he wrote 'The fool on the Hill':

'Day after day, alone on a hill, the man with the foolish grin is keeping perfectly still'..

It's a song about a loner, an outcast, someone who, disregarded by all, sits alone quietly looking, noticing.

'the fool on the hill sees the sun going down and the eyes in his head see the world spinning round...'

But as far as I'm concerned, he wrote it for my Uncle Joe. Not that Paul McCartney ever met my Uncle Joe you understand, but just because it describes him so perfectly.

'And nobody wants to know him, they can see that he's just a fool'

Nobody wanted to know Joe but mom.

You might be wondering how on earth my Uncle has anything to do with ELO. It's a fair question. If there are no patterns to be found in the chaos, if we are really adrift on the winds of purposeless chance, there isn't any connection at all.

The fact is, Joe used to work at a factory in Tile Cross called 'EPE', and for a time, Jeff Lynne happened to work there too – I think he was an apprentice. Anyway, Joe used to give Jeff a lift to and from the 'EPE' every day in his car. Mom was never happy with people taking advantage of Joe and I remember well her confronting him about it: "I hope he's going to pay your petrol money for going out of your way every day," Joe replied firmly that Jeff had promised him "When I make my first million Joe, I'll see yer all right." I suppose it's the sort of remark that's just forgotten – but I believe that God heard it and he didn't forget, because you see the fact is, Jeff did make his million, and Joe was all right.

Oh – Jeff didn't come riding down Briddsland Road with a cheque made out to Joe. – The connection wasn't that visible, and it doesn't need to be: Jeff gave me a job with his group; I bought my mom's house; and mom, well she looked after Joe – right up until the day he died.

THREE – BIRMINGHAM BLUES

The City of Birmingham in the mid sixties was a landscape alternating between the scars of German bombs and the grimy Victorian edifices that marked its industrial heritage. Nestling in its underbelly, just outside the heart of the city centre, was the Cedar Club. It had all the attributes of an Al Capone speakeasy: A dingy frontage looking every bit from the outside like a brothel lit by candles, with windows emanating a muted reddy hue around gaps in the curtains.

I walked up and knocked nervously on the door. It responded instantly, swinging open to reveal a Goliath-type figure replete with black tuxedo, bow tie and a countenance of practised menace.

"Hello. Er… I'm here to see Danny King." I said.

"Yeah, and you are…?"

"Dave Morgan."

Without a word, the door swung shut. I hovered on the pavement for a few minutes while spivs with scantily clad girls shuffled past me to be granted immediate recognition and entry into the dark interior. Eventually the door opened again for me:

"Okay" said Goliath, motioning me in through the portal, to the inner sanctum of playboy Valhalla.

It was my first trip into the world of 'night clubs' – a world of drinking and laughter, noisy revelry, easy women and late nights followed by staying in bed until midday…

I don't know quite how I got the job playing guitar with Danny King, he didn't 'audition' me at all. Maybe it was because he liked my songs. Or maybe it was because he found out I owned a Jaguar motor car… just an old Mark 7 you understand, but yes, it was a Jag. (It had been given to me by the man who collided with my J2 van. He had no insurance and no money to pay for the repairs).

No matter the reason I was with Danny King for eight months and we played the Cedar regularly. Soon it was me who could knock the door and be instantly recognised and ushered inside by the ubiquitous Goliaths. It was the 'in' place to be – you could bump into anyone and everyone at the Cedar: Stars and would-be stars, managers, roadies, groupies – they would all be there, mingled in with the freeloaders, pimps and hustlers.

Ten days after joining Danny King, I became the proud owner of yet another Jaguar motor car. The Mark 9 model promised to be a much swisher steed befitting the gangster class I was now rubbing shoulders with. But first it had to be fixed up. I had bought it as a 'write-off' from an insurance company (for £30). It had crash damage to the rear, which had bent the chassis so badly that the rear doors wouldn't open. A friend of mine helped me to repair it. He cannibalised the panels from the old Mark 7 to spruce up the bodywork and then shackled the chassis to a lug set in concrete and drove the Jag forward at high energy again and again until, "Hey presto": he had stretched it enough to be able to open and close the back doors!

We used to drive in that Jag to Alex's pie stand, outside Snow Hill station in Birmingham, and munch our steak and kidney pies whilst sat in the sumptuous leather seats. It was luxury! The pie went on the little walnut drop-down tables built into the dashboard and seat backs, while the plastic cup full of hot tea sat in the chromium well provided. Just what the makers of Jaguar cars had in mind when they designed it – a couple of dead beats having a take-away meal at Alex's and covering the inside with pastry flakes. Alex's pie stand, like the Cedar club, was a place where, if you stayed long enough, you would be sure to meet every 'face' in town. Sooner or later in the middle of the night they would turn up, on their way back home from gigs.

Germany

Danny King's group sort of fell apart when the organist got arrested at a gig one night... There was something about stolen equipment being found in his inventory. Anyway, shortly after the dust had settled from that fracas I joined a group called 'Blaises,' an attempt at putting together a local super-group by manager Arthur Smith. The local scene however, was soon mercifully released from 'Blaises' as they were extracted out of it and sent to Germany for a month. After all, the Beatles had shown that a stint in Germany was the way to mega-success...

Our group transport was an old ambulance recently retired from service. It was more like a baby charabanc with windows along the side, big comfy seats, and a sleepy soft suspension that imbibed an undulating motion as it trundled along, making it feel like you were travelling on a motorised water bed.

On the ferry crossing from Dover to Calais the Captain of the ship – a stern looking Danish man – took exception to the Ambulance sign still displayed in a lighted vent in the roof of the cab. He gave us a tin of white paint and ordered us in broken English to paint over it before he would let us off his ship. He must have dropped out a word about our unsociable presence to the Gendarmes at Calais because they promptly impounded us, and our ambulance – locking us inside a giant shed for several hours before repatriating us back to England on the same ship.

We spent the night in our ambulance in the car park of Dover harbour and the next morning booked passage on a ferry to Ostend. We hoped the Belgians would be more obliging to us than the French had been, and they were – they let us in without mass arrest, imprisonment or even the suggestion of garrotting anyone.

Our invasion of Europe finally secure, we set course in a somewhat humbled fashion for Germany, bobbing our way across the motorway system through the day and night to arrive at Hannover very early one morning. We found the club where we were booked to play – the Savoy – and looked at it in horror. It was a dump, an old converted cinema, with gaily coloured posters pinned to battered, shabby walls of peeling stucco. We peered through the grey dawn at the scene before us and, in our slightly comatosed, half-asleep condition, made daft jokes about it. Raucous laughter ricocheted through the ambulance as, surveying the state of buildings adjoining the club, one of the group pointed to a desolate outhouse with bars at the windows and said:

"Hey look, there's the hotel where we'll be staying."

Sometime later a cleaner came and let us into the club. We were shown to our quarters – Yes it was the building we had all been laughing about earlier.

We played at the Savoy in Hannover for three weeks, five spots per night, sleeping and living in the concrete bowels of our 'hotel' which had a star rating lower than Colditz. The organ player broke his leg, the singer caught crabs and the drummer had his leg bitten into by a German girl after an enormous fight broke out in the ambulance as we were taking some girls home one night.

After Hannover, we moved to Brunswick for a week – or Braunschweig as it was rendered in the native tongue. We played on a stage that was about three foot wide and fifty foot long – All stood in a line sandwiched against the wall, like suspects in a police line-up.

Across the other side of the club, behind the bar, stood the proprietor: An enormous portly German with a playful, slightly psychopathic manner. He developed a penchant for conducting us from where he stood across the room, employing a system of easily understood hand gesticulations interspersed with a show of his ample knuckles and his best expression of menace. That was his way of telling us to turn down.

Using this orchestral semaphore system, one night he gradually lowered the volume of 'Blaises' until we were turned completely off! – the drummer was tapping gently on the sides of his drum, the singer was just whispering and the only other sound to be heard in the club was our plectrums strumming across dead strings. All our eyes were glued to the owner as he beamed child-like, head raised to the ceiling like a music lover lost in rapture. Then suddenly he recomposed himself into a glare of Wagnerian anger, his jaw sticking out and his face contorting into a raging passion as his hands rose up from the bar-top motioning us to increase the volume... Bit by bit, with hands and fists, he had us get louder.. and louder, and louder, and louder, and even louder still! – Until the noise in the little club was excruciating, and we were thrashing our instruments like drunken dervishes while he stood like a warrior king on a hillside, his arms punching the air in a rage of victorious ecstasy. Yes he was quite a character.

'Blaises' came back from Germany and later went to Turkey before folding in the late spring of 1967. But more about that later…

Ugly's

"What?" mom said horrified, when I told her I was going to join a group called 'The Ugly's'.

Singer Steve Gibbons called up out of the blue one day to ask would I be interested in joining him and his group with the zany name of 'Ugly's'. I went to see them play at the Hen and Chickens in Langley. Yes, they were a tad unusual – and not the slightest bit ugly. Steve performed every song with a voluminous show of theatrical gestures, acting out the lyrics in a deliberate melodrama, something I had not seen done before. For one song he came on with an enormous long brass instrument – at least I think it was an instrument – at any rate he blew down it and with his characteristic show of pomp and circumstance, made appropriate noises to the song 'And the Squire blew his horn' – one of The Ugly's records. All this was quite a novelty to me at the time.

Jim Holden, the drummer, came up to me in the break and spoke as if my becoming an 'Ugly' was a done thing: "I'm glad you'll be joining us Dave. We can talk about things we have in common – like the war for instance!" – a reference to the fact that both he and myself were older than the rest of the group.

The Ugly's were a one-off. Steve was, and still is, a most colourful and charismatic performer with a wonderful voice and a way of expressing himself visually that then, and now, is a treat to behold. I always thought he had 'star' written all over him, but Steve was to make only one incursion into the British hit parade, in the late 70's, with the Chuck Berry song 'Tulane'. Such is rock 'n' roll.

Richard

The 59 Club was a sleazy subterranean cellar in the centre of Birmingham, a setting no doubt inspired by the success of the Cavern club in Liverpool. I went in there one night and immediately noticed the young guy playing the huge semi-acoustic guitar on stage with the group. It wasn't just the guitar that caught my attention, unusual as it was, it was the chords he was playing – I had never seen anything like it! His hand was stretched across the fret board, contorted into voluptuous strange shapes that were definitely not out of my Bert Weedon guitar book. That was the first time I met Richard Tandy, the guitarist with the group 'The Chantelles'.

"What were those chords you were playing"' I asked him after being introduced.

I got to know Richard after that and soon became aware that when it came to dedication to music, he was in another league to me. When he was out of work, he would sit at home day after day playing the piano, practising scales and maybe learning a Bob Dylan song. (He loved Dylan's stuff, as did I). But I was astonished at his patience.

I quickly discovered that Richard could add something worthwhile to any song I could invent. He is a great *busker* – able to pick up the thread of a song and produce an accompaniment off the top of his head, whether on guitar or keyboard. Nowadays, busking seems to have become something of a lost art (if it is an art), but back then we were forever busking. I would take a new song around to him and it would fall together with hardly any rehearsing. We would record it on Richard's B&O recorder in the front room of his mom's house. Yes, if I'm ever asked "who is the best musician you've ever played with" I'd have to say it is Richard.

Carl Wayne

The pie stand had closed early for some reason. We looked out of steamed up car windows at its deserted facade in despair.

"Oh no, I'm starving. What're we gonna do?" someone said.

"Let's go to the Cedar Club for a chip butty" suggested Charlie.

"The Cedar club? Don't be daft. You can't get a chip butty at a night club!"

"Yes you can'" chuckled Charlie. "Just watch me."

So that's what we did. We drove down to the Cedar and installed ourselves at one of the tables opposite the stage, in the dimly lit gulley that passed for a restaurant, and watched with glee as Carl Wayne ordered chip butties for us all. The waiter smirked politely, scribbled something on his pad and disappeared inside the kitchen. We pulled faces and giggled expectantly and after a short while the waiter re-emerged with a tray from which he began to serve us with exaggerated decorum and broken English:

"There you are sir,… Enjoy your meal.." – Giant doorstep pieces of bread cut into sandwich blocks spread thick with butter and in between – chips. Glorious!.

Yes chip butties at the Cedar Club became part of the folk lore. That and the obligatory race through deserted night streets. It was the thing to do for some reason. The last one to get there was... well the last one to get there, what more need I say? 'There' might be someone's house, or a club, or some venue of perceived importance to lads who perceived only glory as really important. Glory with a bit of outrage and silliness thrown in.

Yes it was the age of being gloriously and outrageously silly. Charlie had a different take on glory to me though, and one of the more outrageous things he used to do was to smash up a television set on stage: I thought having a Beatle haircut was revolutionary, but destroying a television set? Surely there must be a law against that? – Isn't it sacrilege or something?

The way Charlie did it was akin to a religious experience. I know, I was part of the congregation at the Belfry – a posh hotel in the Sutton Coldfield countryside. Carl Wayne was on stage with his recently formed super-group, the 'Move'. The music had evaporated into a long solo with Roy Wood studiously thrashing his Fender and Trevor Burton standing like an angry sphinx, lasing the audience with his steely glare while at stage front, Carl was fixed into a mean pose and lost in apparent meditation. All the time lights were flashing (yes, that was a new thing too, before the name 'strobing' was ever invented) and at the back, Bev Bevan industriously flailed away at his drumkit. I do believe I saw the slightest flicker of a grin pass Bev's face as a roadie shuffled by holding a table followed by another roadie – Upsy, the chief roadie no less – grasping a Television set. The table was placed ceremoniously at stage front and the tele placed on top. An altar and a sacrifice...

The crowd gasped – Carl Wayne had picked up an axe from somewhere and was circling around the table like a lion stalking a downed gazelle, going around and around, first one way and then the other for what seemed like ages until...

Suddenly he exploded. Wallop. The wooden cabinet split apart. More blows. Bang. The tube went with a tinkly popping sound... Charlie was lost in manic rage. He smashed the axe down again and again while the crowd, me included, stood transfixed in the symbology of it all – a public execution by a crazed axe-man! Finally the ritual was complete and the roadies returned to retrieve the pieces of the TV set. I think the Move finished the song but I don't really remember. Maybe I was being treated for shock or something? I just remember thinking afterward "How very strange. What does it all mean…?"

Well of course, it meant that 'The Move' were bent upon *moving* up and out of Birmingham; the Midlands; anywhere remotely provincial, and stepping up into the centre stage of our universe – London, the capital of the music world. With the help of their new manager, media locust Tony Secunda, Charlie had set the Move on to a trajectory that would make them a household name. It was a fact that unfolded before our Brummie eyes.

And in between these goings on, we recorded loads of my songs, mainly at my mom's house. Charlie was an honoured visitor, one of the few amongst my musician pals to gain mom's unreserved approval. She'd make sure the table cloth was clean when Charlie was coming to visit, and he always paid her special attentions too. We never spent a long time on the recordings. It was never a job, always something like:

"I'd like to play that song to somebody Dave. Let me have a tape of it." And me replying:

"Oh, I don't have a decent demo of it yet." And Charlie would say:

"Right, I'll pop around at so-and-so time and we'll record it." That was the way it happened. I would be frantic with care about every syllable and crotchet but Charlie would just turn up and sing my song, and in three minutes it would all be over. Mom would make a cup of tea and be fussing all over him while I was scribbling the name of the song on a tape box, with a note that Carl had sung it.

Life in the Brum beat era was like one long fairground ride. The lights dazzled, the music blared and the carousel kept spinning while all of us with something to sing or write were sucked up into its vortex of beautiful promise.

Something

True to their promise, the Move became a hit group in 1967 when their song 'Night of Fear' sped into the British charts. It happened while I was in Spain with The Ugly's. – It was the only time I ever got asked to play lead guitar, and that was only because Willy Hammond (the lead guitarist) had told us that his mom wouldn't let him go to Spain with us!

The following year, Carl Wayne – 'Charlie' – started taking serious interest in my songs and soon became a regular visitor at my home in Tile Cross. My mom thought the world of him, for years she would save all the newspaper articles about him.

Charlie and I became pals and we used to play chess at his house until the early hours. We went through phases where he would win every game, and then I would win every game. But it was always one more game for the 'decider' until we were too tired to carry on.

I had been trying to compose an entertaining song with a nice simple tune and I came up with 'That Certain Something'. Unusually for me, it wasn't written for anyone or anything in particular, it was just about the flow of life; – the search for that certain something that you can't describe, but like Steve McQueen said in the horror movie 'The Blob' – 'you'll know it when you see it!'

I played it to Charlie on guitar and he picked up on it straight away, shortening the title to 'Something'. Then in the summer of '68, Charlie told me he was going to do it with the Move. They recorded it with a string arrangement (a new departure for them) and by November, it was a toss-up which would be the A side for the new single release – my song 'Something' or Roy Wood's 'Blackberry Way'.

On 13 November, Charlie and I were in London, at the offices of 'Galaxy' – Don Arden's management company. Don Arden was the Move's manager (Tony Secunda was manager when they became famous, but now we are a little further downstream). Don was a short stubby man who seemed to revel in promoting his legendary renown as a gangster – you could call him 'The Don' and he wouldn't get offended. The godfather angle was probably good for business!

(Nowadays it's probably easier to identify Don Arden as being Ozzie Osbourne's father-in-Law)

He took me by the arm and led me to the window overlooking Denmark Street. The oft-quoted story of him hanging somebody out of a window until they swore to sign a contract, wafted before my mind's eye, but thankfully he just wanted to talk where we couldn't be overheard:

"David, I want to ask you something: You know 'The Move' really need a hit with this next record. Which of the two songs is in your opinion, the most commercial track? – which one is likely to make the most money?"

What a question! I thought hard for a moment while he stared at me. Of course I wanted my song to be on the A side.... but something told me the accurate answer to the question was Roy's song.

I don't know if Don took notice of my advice but the fact is a few weeks later 'Blackberry Way' was climbing up the charts, and by the following February, it was at number one. My song was on the B side and that was good for me also, at least financially. The publisher gave me an advance of £500 for it, a small fortune at the time. I remember I banked it and then withdrew the lot in cash so that I could go and open a new account closer to where I lived. Coming out of the bank I dropped the lot in the street. It was like a scene from 'The Gold of the Sierra Madre': I was on my hands and knees in the road, eyes bulging with avarice, competing with the wind for dominion over the rebellious green tablets trying to make their escape down the Washwood Heath Road.

'The Move' recorded one further song of mine: 'This Time Tomorrow' but before that was to happen, other dramas came into focus...

Trevor Burton and drummer Bev Bevan got into an argument one night while they were on stage in Germany. According to how Charlie related it to me, Trevor threw his bass guitar at Bev. Now Bev is quite a muscular bloke, and when he stood up and grabbed the nearest weapon to hand – his side drum which Upsy, the roadie, had nailed to the stage to stop it moving, he picked it up with such venom that the stage planking came up too. He then proceeded to project the whole rig with due vigour at Trevor. The crowd thought it was all part of the act and they cheered and whooped with delight... Meanwhile as the two disappeared off stage, chasing each other with various items of stage furniture, Charlie and Roy were left to continue the song alone, and when the curtain fell that night, that was the end of the Move with Trevor Burton in it.

I was aghast with shock when Charlie told me about it, but his next statement floored me even more:

"My choice is for you to join the Move to take Trevor's place. But keep it under your hat for now, when all the contractual stuff is sorted out with Trevor, I'll let you know more."

And a couple of weeks later, as 'Blackberry Way' was climbing the last rungs of the top ten ladder, Charlie did formally ask me to join the Move on bass guitar. It was a great opportunity and I told him I would think about it. And think about it I did.

I had been with Steve Gibbons in The Ugly's for eighteen months and I liked playing with the Ugs. To complicate matters, my mate Richard Tandy had just joined on piano and Steve had told me that there was even talk of Trevor Burton now joining us (!!) and of the group being re-formed and going for the big time in a completely new direction.

But in the end the thing that made up my mind were the powerful forces I saw in spin around 'The Move'. Maybe it came from having the Don as manager. It was the flavour of it, the aroma – the cool ambience of cut-throat power that would ride rough shod over anything. It was being in a pressure-cooker stoked by values I wanted to avoid. And as the saying goes: *If you can't stand the heat, get out of the kitchen*' Or in my case, don't go in the kitchen in the first place.

Yes I felt I belonged more in Steve's easy-going world than in the little I had seen of the world that the Move inhabited. I suspected also that my songs were better suited to The Ugly's style and decided to take my chances with them. So, I turned down the offer of a job in the famous 'Move'.

Interestingly, before I was asked, Jeff Lynne was asked the same question (Roy wanted him in the group, Charlie wanted me!). Jeff turned it down because he too wanted to stay with the group he was with – the Idle Race.

The upshot of all this is that Trevor Burton did indeed join The Ugly's – as the lead guitarist. Willy Hammond got sacked to accommodate him, and under Trevor's input and influence, Steve had agreed that the group would have a new manager, Tony Secunda. I winced when the news came in. I had escaped the net of Don Arden only to be caught in the snare of Tony Secunda, himself a legend with his aggressive confrontational style. (He once devised an advertising campaign which implied that the Prime Minister, Harold Wilson, was having an affair. The ensuing legal battle cost 'The Move' all the royalties to a top ten hit). But by now I couldn't back out. The job with 'The Move' had gone to someone else (Rick Price). When you've made your bed you've got to lie in it.

Being sacked from The Ugly's was the best thing that ever happened to Willy Hammond. He went off and joined the Air Force and this metamorphosed into a distinguished career in the foreign office, with many adventures of international gravity, the substance of things that set the exploits of the entertainment business into dim insignificance.

The new group with new direction, new ethos and new manager, needed a new name. Needless to say with Tony Secunda involved, it had to hit you square between the eyes, and if it could be inflammatory too, so much the better. The new banner was unfurled and I found myself in the group named 'Balls' – the most aptly named group I have ever been in. It was a disaster from the word go.

The Dish

The Birmingham group scene had ways to deter anyone from taking themselves too seriously. It was all to do with the way you presented your self, or were presented by others. An unearned or artificially enhanced notoriety could result in you being labelled as *flash*, which was akin to having a notice board strung around your neck warning that you carried a communicable disease. Yes, the Flash Squad was ever on the prowl to bring you back down to earth...

In particular, anything produced by the publicity men – posters, pictures or promotional stuff – could be quickly translated into the fodder of jokes and put-downs. The more splendid the accolade, the more caustic was the ridicule to be heaped upon whoever was its hapless beneficiary. I suppose it was the way we all kept each other in check, although nobody ever said it was a rule, nevertheless a rule it was. Anyone perceived to be pompous or remotely pretentious was fair game to be tarred and feathered.

In the mid sixties there was a group called 'The Walker Brothers' – two good looking American guys who, before they broke into the big time, had a third member, a Brit named Jim O'Neill. Jim came from Birmingham and being a rather good looking chap himself, was chosen to complete the perfect triangle of brotherly talent. Now the press – the newspapers and magazines of the day – clawed avidly for photographs of these three handsome 'Walker Brothers' and their faces beamed at us frequently from popular publications. It was a magazine – actually the teen magazine 'Fabulous' – that was to reshape, reinvent, indeed rename Jim, when it published a full-page spread of the heavenly trio with the caption below obsequiously labelling him as: '…the DISHY Jimmy O'Neill'.

It was a point of sedition that was not to be lost on the watchful organs of the Flash Squad...

Sometime later Jim left 'The Walker Brothers' and moved back to Birmingham to become a long-standing member of The Ugly's.

So when I got to join the group in July 1967, singer Steve Gibbons introduced bass player Jim to me simply as: "The Dish." When I enquired further – "What does that mean, The Dish?" – I was greeted with a cavalcade of chuckles and guffaws from the group and even 'The Dish' himself would only proffer me a wry smile by way of explanation. It had become his name. But eventually, I got to learn the story of the lineage and nativity of the noble house of Dish, birthed as it was by the copy-writer of a teenage girl's magazine.

I soon got to meet Jim's sister Kathy, and as far as I was concerned she was a lot dishier than brother Jim. I went out with Kathy O'Neill for several years and we are still friends now. Kathy would herself sometimes address Jim by his adopted name, albeit as a soldier would use a bayonet, calling him 'The Dish' to administer the coup de grace at some suitable juncture of family disunion.

I wrote many songs for Kathy but the one I always remember her by is 'Mary Colinto'. The song became a sort of local hit, being played by many Birmingham groups, including The Ugly's who made a record of it which was all set for release in early 1969 before the group disbanded to form 'Balls'.

Swedish Baroness

And then there was Gabrielle, the Swedish baroness, exiled from her inheritance to live amongst the commoners of Birmingham – in the suburb of Rednal in fact, where she worked as a seamstress and made all the clothes for The Ugly's. Ah, how she entertained us with her Nordic accent and fine sweeping movements of her slender frame as she modelled her psychedelic garments and wove her dream of one day being repatriated to the beautiful snow-capped mountain redoubt, the castle and the family heirloom, all hers by right and you'd better not doubt it, stolen from her by wickedness and subterfuge. And later, much later, how we learned incredulously that she was neither Swedish nor baroness, and this fact along with her true accent (which turned out to be as common as ours) were laid upon us like the sodden plot of some bar-room play. Yes, Gabrielle was one of the characters who made the sixties what they were for us, a voyage of pure discovery on the good ship Whimsy.

Meditations

The Beatles were my idols and in the late sixties they became devotees of the Maharishi Mahesh Yogi – the 'transcendental meditation' guru from India that they themselves had transcended into superstar status for a short while in 1968. It was really due to the fact the Beatles had thrown their lot in with the Maharishi that I had a go at it. After all, if they said it was okay, they must know what they're talking about!

Along with Steve Gibbons and his girl friend, I drove to London one day for a TM seminar in a hotel. Afterwards I put my name down to be 'initiated'.

A week or so later, I received my mantra at a short ceremony in Birmingham, not from the Maharishi but one of his faithful cohorts, an English actor whose name escapes me now. With my mantra enabled, I would drift off into the big blue nowhere – it was quite novel for awhile... You meditate on your mantra until it, you, and everything else becomes a meaningless flubber and you enter into that big blank of perfect nothingness. I thought it must be a sort of modern method of praying but later on I discovered that prayer is more of a dialogue and nothing like meditation. Certainly nothing like the void that Transcendental Meditation pointed to as the ultimate goal, the ointment to sooth the ills of our modern world. For I found inside is not like a void, but more like an open bucket waiting to be filled, longing in fact to be filled. I think it was G.K Chesterton who said 'If you believe in nothing, you believe in everything that comes your way'.

Anyway, the Beatles soon seemed to lose interest in the Maharishi, and so did I. Only George Harrison carried on with his affinity for the Indian culture, music and finally, religion.

Years later, I watched the Beatles Anthology and saw clips from 1968 of John, Paul, George and Ringo with the Maharishi at his retreat in Rishikesh, India. Many other stars of stage and screen were in attendance, following him around as if attached by a hidden lanyard to his billowing white robes – a princely entourage indeed.

Paul McCartney cut in to reminisce on camera about an incident that happened:

The Maharishi was about to go off in a helicopter and there were three seats on board, one for the pilot, one for the Maharishi, and a spare seat for someone else. A gaggle of devotees cloistered close to him as he moved in his characteristic unhurried gait toward the helicopter. John Lennon was one of them. Sure enough, as the Maharishi stepped in the machine he turned to John and offered him the spare seat.

Some time later, after he got back, Paul quizzed him, ribbing him about it at the same time:

'Hey John, I saw you pushing yourself forward so you could get that seat on the helicopter to be with the Maharishi. How come it was so important to you to go with him?'

John replied: 'Well, I thought when we were alone together, he might drop something out – you know, tell me the secret or something.'

'And did he?'
'Did he what?'
'Tell you the secret?'
'Nah, he never said anything!'

To me the wonderful irony about all this is that there's John Lennon, clutching at straws from the hand of the Maharishi Mahesh

Yogi, while at the same time there's me, along with most everybody else in my world, hanging on every word John Lennon said because we thought HE had the secret!

Balls

'Balls' lasted for one whole month. For me it did anyway. The group was formerly inaugurated on Monday February 3 1969. It was a heady time all round. Just two days before this I had been offered the job of playing bass guitar with 'The Move'. On that day they were Number 4 in the UK singles charts with 'Blackberry Way', which had my song 'Something ' on the B side. As Carl Wayne wanted me to join his group he didn't like the idea of me going off with Trevor and Tony Secunda. He had even arranged a flat at Streetly (a very posh area North of Birmingham) where I could shack up and write songs in peace.

Meanwhile, Tony Secunda, manager of the new creation 'Balls', had arranged for his new group to be salted away in the countryside of the New Forest. He had a pal named Tiny. (Yes, you've guessed it – Tiny was huge!) He ran the pub in the village of Fordingbridge, Hampshire, right in the middle of the New Forest. Just a short drive out of the village, Tiny had found a bungalow where Secunda's new group could be uninterrupted as they pursued their quest for pop stardom in fine English style, as country bumpkins.

I had made the decision to stay with Steve Gibbons and so I moved down to Fordingbridge. It was a special place – New Forest Donkeys came roaming in the kitchen of the little wooden bungalow that was our humble habitation and flagons of country cider were a standing order on shopping day.

I drove back to Birmingham one Sunday in late February and called Carl. He announced to me that he wanted to record a song of mine called 'One Month in Tuesday' (which went by the affectionate nom de plume 'Corky' on account of the fact it began: 'Corky wrote today…'). I telephoned Trevor to tell him about this – for me, good news. He was hopping mad about it, suggesting that Charlie was up to no good. I spoke to Charlie again and a little later he called me back to tell me he had called Tony Secunda, and there was no problem at all about him recording one of my songs.

Secunda was strangely and uncharacteristically ambivalent it seemed…

When I returned to Fordingbridge on Monday, I learned that Trevor had left abruptly for London after the phone call the day before. He re-appeared with Denny Laine late on Tuesday the 25th and the two of them didn't have very much to say but I remember they did play all night at a very loud volume. Just why Denny Laine had come along, seemed to have sinister overtones to me, and the next day, I spoke to Steve Gibbons about it. He didn't know why he'd come either and was bothered about it himself. It seemed to portend a change of line-up… We both decided we needed to speak to Trevor about it but when we did, he flatly denied that any change in the group was afoot:

"Absolutely not" Trevor said, shaking his head.

"Denny is just sitting in with us because his thing has fallen through in London." He was quite emphatic about it. Steve and I were re-assured.

The new super group lurched on for another week. Rehearsals were, I guess I would describe them as undisciplined. The music was almost exclusively interminable 12 bar blasts that went on for hours, the archetypal rock n roll groove. I didn't much like the groove and I didn't much like the politics – increasingly there was a pervading atmosphere of intrigue around the place. Then on Tuesday 4 March, Trevor and Steve Gibbons took me to one side. Trevor said to me:

"This band ain't happening!" I felt a certain relief to hear that. At last somebody had put it into words. He continued:

"…and er… We have decided that er… you, – that is you and er… Richard… well.., you don't fit!"

That was it! I looked at Steve. He wore a grimace of resigned displeasure, like somebody who had signed up for the parachute regiment and now wished he hadn't. But it was too late.

I could sense it had been ordained from on high by the master tactician himself – Tony Secunda, together with Trevor and Denny, with Steve's agreement tacked on.

I baled out immediately and I think Richard left the next day.

Keith Smart also left the group around this time, although I am not sure precisely when. I do remember being surprised to hear that he, like us, was back in Birmingham. Keith had been Trevor's closest pal. What can you say? That's rock n roll.

Much later, Steve himself left 'Balls' and came back to live in Birmingham. For a long time he was engaged in trying to untangle himself from the web of contractual obligations that now tied him to Tony Secunda and his 'Ball's project. Knowing that I had a similar experience with Lou Reizner, he confided in me about his situation and asked if I would go with him to London the next time he met with Secunda. Accordingly, one day we found ourselves heading down the M1 in my Mini-Cooper to meet with Tony Secunda in his swish flat in Kensington Gardens.

The meeting with Secunda went on several hours. I was in the room with them both, sat on an adjacent sofa like a United Nations observer adjudicating at a massacre. Secunda made no play at keeping most of what was said confidential, only occasionally would he lean forward and whisper something to Steve, out of my earshot. I don't recall any vestige of resolution being reached. Secunda always had a knack of directing the conversation in such a way that he could make you feel you had gained something of galactic value and importance while at the same time you would be vaguely aware you were witnessing all your hopes and dreams disappearing down the plughole at a rapid rate of knots! Steve had one eye on the time because he had a gig in Birmingham later that evening. As the meeting dragged on, eventually Steve turned to me and announced that time was up – he had to leave.

I said I would go and get the car and bring it outside to the front. "Okay" said Steve, as Tony opened the door for me.

The single road into Kensington Gardens from Kensington High Street split quickly into a closed loop cuddled by big ornate terraced houses. The roadway was bedecked either side with parked cars and between these, there was only room for one vehicle to pass in the middle. I got to my car, and by the time I had driven around the loop to Tony's flat, Steve and Tony were waiting for me on the pavement, heads down in conference together. The discussions had obviously revived at the last minute!

I pulled up alongside. Steve noticed me and slowly shuffled sideways to the passenger door, while embroiled in the dialogue with Tony. He slowly got in my car and wound down the window. Tony knelt down on the pavement beside my little Mini-Cooper (which had a specially lowered suspension making it even lower than normal). Tony thrust his head inside the window and continued talking to Steve at a breathless pace while the only other sound that could be heard was the gentle purr of my Mini-Cooper at tick-over. For quite a few minutes, I sat listening while these high powered discussions went on beside me but then suddenly, I noticed the background ambience had been disturbed by a metallic clacking sound and, looking in my mirror, I saw it was from a taxi that had pulled up behind us. It was waiting for us to move on. I fidgeted nervously while Tony just carried right on talking. About half a minute went by and there was a 'honk from the taxi's horn. Steve registered the situation with a glance over his shoulder, but Tony never missed a beat. He just carried right on talking. Another half a minute elapsed and then the taxi driver let out a longer 'Beeeep'. Nothing. No reaction at all from Secunda. I was like a nervous pigeon, eyes darting between Steve, Secunda and the rear-view mirror, where a pallor of mounting rage could be seen rising on the taxi driver's face. But Tony, acting oblivious to it all, just carried right on talking. Another half minute and the taxi driver began hitting his horn repeatedly 'Beep', Beep', 'Beep', 'Beep', like a burglar alarm going off. Secunda tutted, raised his head up out of the car and shouted to the taxi driver: "Hey, will you be quiet. I can't *hear* him!" and immediately put his head back inside the car and continued talking with Steve as if nothing had happened. Behind me in the mirror, I could see the door of the taxi open and the driver stepping out to discuss the matter with us in a more intimate way. That was it.

"Steve, we have got go!" I said commandingly, thrusting the Mini into gear. "See you Tony" I shouted as he mumbled something about "Hold on, what's the problem man?" I dropped the clutch and we sped off.

Jeff Silvas and the Four Strangers 1963-64

It was the age when groups wore matching uniforms. Ours were posh red tuxedos with a dash of silver on the lapels. Front man Jeff wore white.

Above Jeff Sylvas & the 4 Strangers playing at the Meadway pub. From left: Bill Miller, John Panteney, Jeff Silvas, myself. The fourth Stranger - bass player Ray Hammond - is out of shot to the right.

The final version of the 4 Strangers posing for the camera circa 1965 Left to right: drummer Alan Bennett, myself, Ray Hammond and Bill Miller.

Jeff Silvas and the Four Strangers

Left
Jeff Silvas and the Four Strangers at an unknown gig (could be Solihull Civic Hall?)

Left
a session shooting publicity photos in a field near Marston Green, on the outskirts of Birmingham.

Photographs by the manager, Ralph Hitchcock

Chantelles 1965

I took this shot of The Chantelles stopping for a cuppa at the Motorway services on the way to play an audition at the Marquee in London. From the left: John 'Pank' Panteney (drums), John Fincham (bass), Ray Hammond (bass No.2 – yes we had two bass guitarists!), Pete Gilbert (van driver and roadie) and Jeff Lynne.

Playing at the NCO club, Incirlick Air Base, Turkey. The drummer is Keith Smart.

Double exposure
Blaises, 18 March 1967

An open-air show at Incirlick which was televised across the base.

Above Bass player Bob Doyle and me on stage with Blaises.

Left: Corky and daughter Deniz visit Tile Cross, August 1968.

Left: Pic taken in Charlie's back garden for a Birmingham Mail write-up on Carl Wayne's new song publishing company - 'Penny Music'. Richard and I were to be the flagship 'writers' for this venture.

Mary Colinto - Jim's sister Kathy O'Neill.

Mary Colinto is the title of a song I wrote in 1968 which became a sort of local hit, played by many Birmingham groups. It was recorded by the Ugly's for the CBS label but not released due to the group disbanding to form Balls.

Danny King & Trevor Burton 1966,
admiring Trevor's new purchase – a Ford Zephyr

The Cedar Club 1968. Trevor Burton, Richard Tandy, myself and Carl Wayne.

The Ugly's 1967-68.
Below playing at 'The Station' in Selly Oak, Birmingham.
From left: Willy Hammond, Steve Gibbons, Jim Holden, myself.

Above: Steve, Willy and myself lounging on the patio of the Kings Head pub. We are there for a business meeting with The Ugly's manager John Singer.
Left, an earlier version of the Ugs with me on rhythm guitar.

The Dish. Jimmy O'Neill (centre) with Steve Gibbons and drummer Jim Holden.

Torremolinos, Spain, 1967
Steve, myself and Jim Holden

The Ugly's 1969. A pic of the last Uglys' line up before evolving into Balls and becoming extinct! At the back: Richard Tandy, myself, Steve Gibbons. At front: Willy Hammond and Keith Smart.

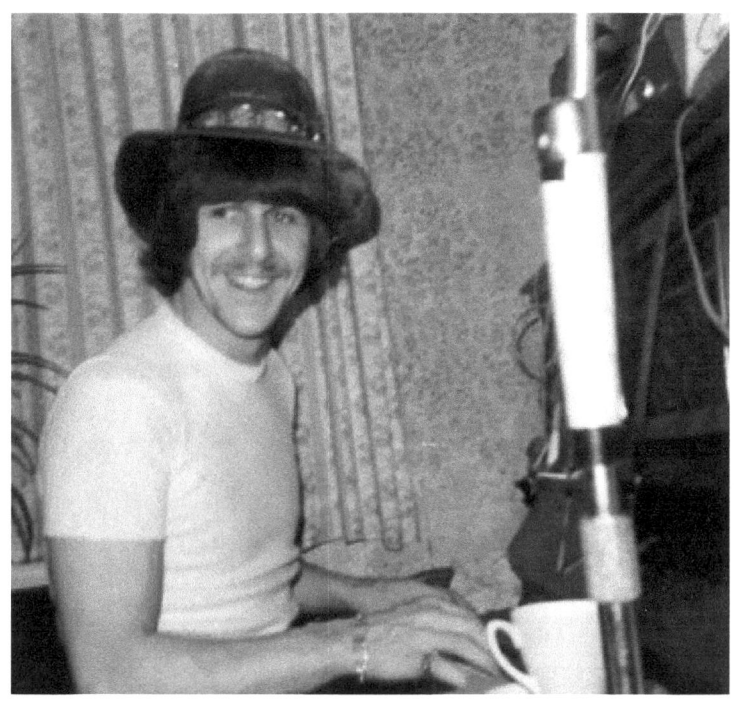

'Blackberry Way' hit the number one spot in February 1969. The B side is my song 'Something' Here Charlie - Carl Wayne - plays piano at my mom's house.

Above Richard strums a guitar in the back of my Mini-Cooper circa 1972.

Below in car park of the old BBC studios in Edgbaston, Birmingham. Left to Right Carl Wayne, Steve Gibbons, Jimmy O'Neil ('The Dish') and roaddies John Lippet and 'Upsy' (John Downing).

The local Fordingbridge paper published this pic of Balls on February 19 1969. From the left: Trevor Burton, Steve Gibbons, Dave Morgan, Keith Smart, Richard Tandy.

The ever faithful Mini Cooper replete with air intake welded into the bonnet by car mechanic pal David Brown, affectionately known as 'Hovis'.

FOUR – SEVENTIES

Big Yank

Lou Reizner was a strapping hulk of a man, bronzed and broad-shouldered, effervescent with that easy optimism that naturally infects Americans and equally naturally, bewilders the British working class, from whence I was begotten.

Lou, proprietor of Reizner Music Inc, had gained an interest in me as a songwriter and travelled to meet me in Birmingham one summer's day in 1970. I picked him up from New Street station and then on the way to my mom's house, he spotted a strange apparition:

"What is that?" he exclaimed.

"Hey Dave, pull over a minute."

I waited in my car outside a showroom for Reliant three-wheelers (!!) while, through the window, I saw Lou squeezing his giant torso into this, the archetypal conveyance of the English poor. It couldn't possibly have had any transportation interest to him, I imagine it was a jaunt of pure daftness, an item of zaniness to turn up in at some Golders Green party.

That day I played Lou all the good songs I had written and soon afterwards, I was invited down to his London offices to talk turkey...

Lou lived in a sumptuous palatial residence in Kensington, right next to the cavalry barracks. The spacious ornate first floor room that was 'the office' had as its main focus an enormous carved wooden desk. Behind the desk, lay French windows, and beyond, a balcony overlooking Hyde Park. All kinds of curios hung on the walls or stood poised in position around the room. A sword hanging in its sheath, an enormous globe gimballed atop its stilted bucket... I dare say each one could tell a tale of being held in regal hands, or of witnessing some august conjunction of the rich and the powerful.

Lou sat at his desk with the trees of Hyde Park swaying behind him while turkey was talked, and a deal was done. He signed me up as both writer and artist, giving me a handsome advance against my songs.

Then after the shortest slice of time, I learned that he had produced an entire album of my songs with a British group called 'Wishful Thinking'. The album was to be called 'Hiroshima', the title of one of the songs. Lou had heard the scratchy demo I had done with Willy Hammond's help on my B&O recorder and zoomed in upon its simple message, but I have to admit I was enormously embarrassed to hear the finished version: Lou himself had done the voiceover, a repeat of the actual broadcast that reported to the world the explosion of an atom bomb over Hiroshima in August 1945.

Shortly afterwards, Lou booked studio time (at Morgan studios, north London) to record an album of me singing my own songs. For a couple of weeks, while this was rehearsed and recorded, I stayed with him at his office-cum-apartment in Kensington. One day he came in from an appointment, installed himself solemnly behind his massive desk and addressed me with all seriousness:

"I've just been to visit my astrologer Dave, and she has told me that the thing I am now working on – that means your music Dave – is going to have great success."

He studied my response, which was a puzzled "Oh!" It hung in silence for a few seconds, like a pregnant question, for I had never before heard of such a weird thing. Someone with the power to divine the future…

He seemed to believe in it but it left me with an uncomfortable feeling and I couldn't wait to get out of the office. How strange it is to recall now, for indeed 'Hiroshima' was for sure *a great success* and yet...

Folk Singer

The advance from Lou enabled me to buy a ticket to the United States where magically, a career as a folk singer began to unfold the very first day I ever set foot on American soil.

But in order to tell you about America, I have to tell you about Turkey first. Yes, you are right, that is the wrong direction completely, but that's rock 'n' roll. Really, it was only going to the land of Caliphs and Minarets that enabled me to get to America. Let me explain...

I was with a group called 'Blaises' and for three months in early 1967 we were resident in south-east Turkey, playing five nights a week at the giant US Air Force base called Incirlick – where Gary Powers had taken off on his fateful U2 spy mission in 1960.

One night we were playing The Officers' Club when a lady caught our attention from the platform – she was easily the most sparkling and vivacious lady on the dance floor:

"See that bird there?" bass player Bob whispered to me while we were playing.

"Yeah, she's mine, lay off" I giggled back.

"Oh yeah?, we'll see about that."

In the break a man came up and complimented me on the way I sang the song 'The Lady is a Tramp'.

"My name is Joe Corcoran" he said, "come over and have a drink with us."

I walked across the dance floor to his table and was introduced to his wife. It was the 'bird' we had been ogling (!!)

"My name is Turkan" she said, explaining that she was in fact Turkish, "but everyone calls me Corky."

Close up I could see how her stunning features had discounted her age, which was only thirty plus, but then, when you are as I was, twenty plus, anyone beyond the next magic threshold inhabited the realm of moms and aunts.

After this first meeting I soon became a regular visitor at the Corky residence in the nearby town of Adana. We became good pals. Yes, pals- don't get any ideas! Although she was beautiful, Corky was always like a surrogate mother to me.

The following year while she was en-route back to America, Corky and her daughter Deniz came to spend a day with me in Birmingham. Before she left, she extended an open invite for me to stay at her home in Glen Burnie, Maryland – if I could ever afford the ticket to get to America, that is.

And so in the autumn of 1970, after recording the album of my songs with Lou Reizner, I found I had both the appetite and the money to take Corky up on her offer.

I landed at New York's JFK airport on 30 October 1970, wide-eyed and jet lagged and carrying an acoustic guitar in a leatherette bag. Waiting for the connecting plane I struck up a conversation with the then-unknown group 'Black Sabbath', who had heard my Brummie accent at the check-in desk. We travelled together to Philadelphia, a stop on the way to Baltimore. I had never met them before, although they were from Birmingham.

Corky was waiting to meet me at Baltimore airport with an enormous welcoming smile and expansive hugs. After installing me in my own room at her house ('boy, my own room! – I never had my own room at mom's house in Tile Cross' I thought!) she drove me around the 'sights' of Glen Burnie and we popped in to the local shopping mall. That's where I met George Richardson, the effervescent manager of one of the shops.

"Oh so you're Corky's friend – Oh, you met in Turkey and you're English, Oh – Wow! – AND you play guitar! – Hey, I run a coffee shop here in Glen Burnie. Why don't you come down?"

He seemed to be describing something other than a retailer of coffee beans, but I'd never heard of the expression –

"What's a Coffee shop?" I asked.

"Oh you know, a place where we all sit round and play music" he replied in the easy, silver manner of the salesman he was, adding that 'tonight' was 'coffee shop' night.

That was how I got to be performing in front of people the very first day I was in America. I played a few songs – some of mine and a Dylan song 'Just Like a Woman'. It went down so well I became a regular at George's Coffee shop before branching out for new horizons.

The horizon that beckoned was in a southerly direction, and I was propelled toward it by a girl I had met (a 'dizzy broad' Corky called her disapprovingly!). Sharon had in mind toasting herself in the Florida sun and away from the freezing Baltimore winter of January 1971. Together we planned a way to get to the sun via the auspices of a drive-away car (that's a car whose owner has jetted on ahead leaving it to be delivered to him. Only in America do such things exist it seems).

It took two and a bit days to ply the 1,200 miles down the eastern states of the Union in our posh 1968 Cadillac Fleetwood that I had been commissioned to deliver to its owner in Miami. In Georgia, we passed a chain gang of convicts at the roadside, hacking at the verge with hoes and shovels while a couple of overfed foremen stood watching... At Daytona, Florida, we drove along the beach – the same hard shoulder of sand stretching for miles where Malcolm Campbell's Bluebird had pushed the world land speed record to over 400 mph in the 30s.

Just north of the city of Miami, in the coastal town of Fort Lauderdale, a little motel caught our eye: the 'Riptides' it said proudly on the high gaudy neon sign. We pulled in and rented a room.

That evening I found myself sitting around the pool beneath the mild tropical winter sky of Florida, strumming my guitar while the motel manager and a couple of other young guys listened. The manager immediately telephoned a friend of his – Ron – who had a late night show on a radio station in Miami (WBUS – 'Magic Bus') and got me to sing down the phone to him.

"Can you go down to the station and do a session for him?" the motel manager asked me.

"When?"

"Now!"

Miami

I spent quite a few late nights at the 'Magic Bus' station with Don the DJ. One time he got me reading the news over the air and I remember stumbling over the pronunciation of places in Vietnam that figured with sinister repetition in the news reports of the time. But the thing I remember most about that little closet of a studio is that that is where I met 'The Bird'.

"Hi" he said, bursting into the room like a politician appearing from behind a curtain. "My name is Warren but everyone knows me as 'The Bird' – I just heard you on my radio and I wanted to come down and meet you in the flesh. So – here I am! Hello!"

"Oh wow, that's nice. Thanks. And yes, hello…"

'The Bird' looked like an American version of Confucius, his spindly frame animated with an elastic swagger bedecked by an ever-ready, knowing smile. Before he had left the studio that night he had offered me a place to stay and in a short order I had moved in with him, becoming the beneficiary of his home, his Volkswagen car, and really everything he had – except his girl friends of course. I had entered into the pot-smoking hippy culture of America, where everything was communal property.

'The Bird' and I became staunch friends and allies. When the album that Lou had recorded was released in America 'The Bird' wrote the sleeve notes for it. He was a sharp, clued-in man always riding on the vim of a contagious optimism. It was also the first time I really got to know Jewish people – Warren was from a Jewish family and not unreasonably, happened to have Jewish friends. I quickly came to appreciate how dexterous and resourceful they all seemed to be, and to understand a little of why they seemed to have such a pre-eminence in business, especially the music business of course.

Somehow, I don't recall just how, I became hitched up to a local music impresario named Steve Stark, and through him, I met up with a singer named Mickey Carroll. When we met, Mickey was sat with two other musicians high up on an elevated balcony overlooking the bar at the Rancher Motel, Miami, playing his guitar and singing and smiling down at us through his Don Juan moustache, while delivering a Vegas ambience of musical cool.

After his set, we went backstage to the changing room. Steve asked me to play him something and the song 'Oh boy I'm cold' climbed out of its pram into instant fame: I had written it in Corky's basement just a couple of weeks before, and when I played it to Mickey Carroll, he gushed superlatives upon it so much that I wafted out of the Rancher Motel on a cloud of pure cotton wool. I guess the reason Steve wanted me to play a song was so that Mickey could vet me. Anyway, I must have passed because soon Steve swung into action as my manager and I had write-ups in the local papers, a TV appearance, and then a spot singing in a bar in south Miami.

During this time I spent a fair few evenings down in the Coconut Groves at Mickey Carroll's house snuggled amongst the trees. We played songs and talked and laughed a lot while his lovely wife Pat plied us with eats and drinks and looked after their toddler.

For some reason I became interested in astrology. Maybe it was because the people I met in Miami seemed to measure everything that happened to them with reference to their star signs. Like many things that took my fancy I dived into it with fanaticism. Soon, I had purchased ephemeris's – tables of the planetary movements – and learned all about stuff like declination, and taught myself how to draw up astrological charts. I thought this was pretty cool and I could foresee a stream of income flowing from my new found expertise. But unlike Lou Reizner's fortune teller, the problem was I knew how to construct the charts but had no idea how to interpret them into predictions or anything of actual practical use.

By now my bar job in South Miami had turned out to be a tougher assignment than it first seemed. Looking back, I remember that my impersonation of some of the grittier performers around didn't go down too well. My flavour of the moment was the Puerto Rican singer Ritchie Havens and his version of Bob Dylan's 'Just like a Woman' – something of an acquired taste for the uninitiated. I hasten to add that my impersonation of me was only marginally better!

Looking Glass

Consequently, before too long I was jobless and somewhat financially embarrassed. In March I saw an ad in the paper for a job playing bass with a group that had some kind of special programme and *lots of work for the right person.* I responded to the ad and met the group 'The Looking Glass' – Randy, Paul, Flick, and after a short audition, Dave from England – me! The programme certainly was special – they had been contracted to do evangelistic concerts at High Schools all over Florida! I had never heard of such a thing. An evangelistic show which combined playing rock 'n' roll and telling people about Jesus.

Paul, the lead guitarist, did most of the talking. They wanted me to have a go. Why I didn't run a mile I can't tell. Maybe something of my childhood experience of asking God into my life allowed me to suspend my cynicism. Or maybe this *spiritual stuff* seemed more accessible amongst these infuriatingly positive Americans. So I tried a scripted piece but quickly found out I was too nervous to say anything of substance over the microphone. I had a complete block about public speaking (something that remained for another 20 years!) I could just about utter the title of the next song but no more. So I concentrated on playing, bought a second hand Fender Precision bass guitar and throughout May and June of 1971, could be found playing with 'The Looking Glass,' sometimes three times a day, to a captive audience of pupils at schools with names like Palmettos Junior High and North Miami High.

I ended up spending a year and a half in America in two visits separated by a short spell back in England in between. On both trips I played with 'The Looking Glass'.

I also appeared as a folk singer but I have to admit I was not wonderful at it. At one place I got booed off. Mind you, the crowd were waiting to see Eric Burden – the next on the bill – at the time. A roomful of seething rhythm and blues fanatics were greeted by *moi*, with feeble acoustic guitar and wobbly voice and they were not amused. It was what you might call a tough assignment.

Return

I made the second trip to America with Geoff Turton. Geoff had been the singer with the Birmingham group 'The Rockin' Berries' who had a massive hit with the song 'He's in town' back in 1964[1]. It transpired that while I was in America, Geoff had a serious girl friend upset, and by the time I got back he was anxious to disappear from the face of the earth for awhile. I guess if he had been a Frenchman he would have joined the Foreign Legion but as it was, going to America was the next best thing. While I was in Birmingham, Geoff and I met up at Richard Tandy's house and, after relating to me his dilemma, asked: "Could I come back with you to America?" Well, I had an apartment in Miami, and contacts for singing out there so I said "Yes, why not?". He played to me some of the songs he had written in the wake of his recent dramas and I could tell straight away his disaster in love had propelled him to compose some great songs (all of those songs later became part of an album he recorded[2]).

We set off for Gatwick and climbed aboard a lovely stretched DC-8 owned by some rogue airline that has long since become extinct. Full of hope and very little cash we landed at JFK and decided the only way we would be able to stay in New York long enough to get transport to Miami organised, was to find someone – preferably a nice young girl – who we could stay with. So we began approaching every suitable looking girl we laid eyes on and asking them

"Do you know somewhere we can stay?" Needless to say the response varied enormously. Some said "No", others said "I'll scream if you don't go away." Finally I remembered I had the telephone number of Marty Machat's office, (Marty was Lou Reizner's attorney in New York). His secretary, Carol Sue Rothstein, answered the phone and I asked her the magic question... Geoff and I duly wound up at Carol Sue's place. (Years later, some of this drama became embedded in the lyric of 'Paradise Garden'. It speaks of falling from a 'thirty story window' and Marty's office was on the 30th floor of a Times Square skyscraper).

From our new base we organised a drive-away car to Miami, and after calling in on Corky at Baltimore, drove down to take up residence in my flat on Biscayne Boulevard. Geoff found a new girl in America and then later back in England he found yet another new love. And this one – Brigitte – he married, and is married to still.

Rum Runner

It was in the seventies that the 'Rum Runner' night club gradually took over from the 'Cedar' as the premier nocturnal hangout for Birmingham's musicians and the like. The 'Rum Runner' could be truthfully described as an underworld joint as it did in fact occupy the entire basement of a disused Victorian workhouse on Broad Street. It was reached by a long alleyway which descended like a rickety slipway from street level down to the club's dimly-lit entrance.

The subterranean world of the 'Rum Runner' was perennially guarded by Big Albert and his team. Like a posse of preying mantis's Big Albert & Co monitored the stream of revellers that passed before their all-seeing gaze with a special eye for their continued eligibility, or otherwise, of the 'Rum Runner's' grace, favour and festivities.

Yes I would describe Albert as a large man and I can tell you that he kept order in the 'Rum Runner' in much the same way that the Romans kept order at the farthest reaches of their empire: by a system of simple, well-understood rules. Albert's rules were so simple that anyone who got to visit the 'Rum Runner' more than once could understand them perfectly:

"You come in here causing trouble and I'll break your neck," he would declare to the crowd waiting at the entrance, an announcement seemingly made to no one in particular but often magically zooming in to spotlight one who, Albert had already divined with his steely glare, was especially in need of that information. Even so, there was no undue malice in his tone, just a matter of fact helpfulness; a description of cause and effect as neutral as a professor explaining the law of gravity to his pupils.

As I became a regular visitor at the 'Rum Runner', I got to witness Albert's rules in action many times: Often this would take the form of a rugby scrum surging through the labyrinths of the club – Albert and his crew motivating a 'trouble-maker' toward the exit like an army of ants would roll a piece of bread toward their nest, the crowd parting before them like the Red Sea as they inexorably progressed their quarry toward the entrance, and the final resting place of all 'trouble-makers,' the cold cobblestones of the alleyway beyond.

I had worked at the Rum before, for four months in 1970 as part of the resident group, 'Fred's Box'. It was just before recording my album with Lou Reizner. Apart from being the name of a group, 'Fred's Box' was actually a piece of electronic wizardry, a sort of prototype guitar effects pedal that guitarist Fred had built. The story, as related to me by Bob Catley, is that the gadget became enshrined as their name one day when they had been casting around looking for something to call themselves, yet I never did get to figure out just why university graduate Howard Williams answered to the name of 'Fred'!

By 1973, Fred had moved on taking his box with him and leaving only the singer Bob Catley remaining from the original line-up. Around him a new 'Fred's Box' had arisen with Tony Clarkin on lead guitar and Kex on drums – a group that before too long, would call itself 'Magnum'.

At the time, the Rum employed two groups to play each night – one to do the early stint from ten to twelve and another to pick up the remainder, until two o'clock and closing time. In addition, the club's owners – the 'Berrows' family (one of whom was later to taste fame as manager of the hit group 'Duran Duran') were employing their night-time musicians as their daytime navvies working to build a new club. It was to be in the ground floor of an office block, a half a mile from the 'Rum Runner', a building that was in the process of being gutted and re-fashioned into the night spot that would be one day be called 'Snobs'.

Through my frequent visitations to the 'Rum Runner', I got offered a job with the other musicians as a labourer at the pubescent 'Snobs' – a prospect I promptly said 'yes' to, being in need of the cash at the time.

And so I spent my days in the summer of 1973 covered in muck and dust along with the other 'Rum Runner' musicians – banging, drilling, humping, fetching and carrying… Still the indecorous work we did is not what I particularly recall. What I remember best is how it became a comedy house of heinous pranks!

I remember the day that drummer Kex found his brand new boots had been pinned to the concrete floor of our makeshift changing room with an industrial gun, and the fact that the same device was used later to nail someone into a toilet (I don't remember who it was).

And the afternoon when Grant (a guitarist in the 'other' band at the Rum) was using a power hammer to excavate a portion of the concrete floor… Now a 'kango' is a noisy thing even when used in the open air, but inside the shell of the new club, the din it made was absolutely deafening. Grant's efforts went on for quite a while until finally, John (bass player from the 'other' band), unplugged Grant's kango, and cut the plug off the lead with a big pair of scissors.

For several minutes choice words of anger were bandied to and fro across the room, Grant arguing he had to get the job done, while John suggested he did it some other time when he wasn't there.

All the rest of us agreed with John.

A veneer of peace descended upon the workplace as Grant laboured to rewire the plug onto the severed power cord. Twenty minutes later it was done and he announced this fact loudly to us all, adding by way of disclaimer for any subsequent damage to eardrums that he would now be continuing with extra fervour and intensity because 'he had to catch up on lost time and get the job done'.

"Oh Grant?" the voice of John sang to him from the other side of the big room.

"Yeah?" said Grant, looking up as he reached to insert his newly wired plug into the socket of the extension lead.

In the distance, John held the far extremity of the coiled extension cable, offering it up like a bouquet of flowers, with its solitary petal, the electric plug dangling limp and helpless, while in his other hand he held the pair of scissors ….

"No, don't do that," pleaded Grant.

"Well, are you going to make that racket with that thing again?" John rasped back firmly.

"You know I've got to get the job done," said Grant, appealing to John's sense of reason.

It was the totally wrong appeal to make at that juncture.

"Okay then," said John impassionate.

The scissors sliced through the wire and the plug fell with a plonk to the ground, and after John and Grant's shouting and our gales of iniquitous mirth had died away we all spent the rest of the afternoon in a state of tranquil harmony, apart from the fumes of Grant's displeasure hovering about us like a grey cloud.

During that stint as a labourer I became pals with Tony Clarkin, the lead guitarist of 'Fred's Box,'

One night after a days' work at 'Snobs', I was in the 'Rum Runner' as usual, standing by the stage watching 'Magnum' playing, when Mr. Berrow came in and spoke with some visible sternness to the bass player (who happened to also be in charge of the musicians working on the new club). The group took an immediate break and disappeared for high-level discussions.

Tony Clarkin reappeared a short time later and came up to me explaining that some administrative chicanery had come to light and the finger of blame had fallen heavily upon their bass-player.

"The gaffer wants him OUT right away" Tony said.

"You play bass, don't you Dave?" he added, more like he was telling me than asking me.

"Yes" I confirmed.

"Do you want the job?"

"Er, yes."

"Right, you're in."

"Oh, er.. great, thanks."

That's how I got to play loud bass guitar for 'Magnum'. I don't recall the instance the group changed its name from 'Fred's Box' but I do remember the new name being Tony's idea.

"What's a magnum?" I asked him.. Of course it was the gun Clint Eastwood used in 'Dirty Harry'.

It was really the genesis of the heavy-metal group who were later to sell many tens of thousands of records and become a cult hit amongst Christendom's head-bangers and leatherwear rockers, under the propulsion of Tony's great songs and guitar playing, but back then they were still just a resident group at a nightclub, playing the flaccid hits of the day and being perpetually told to turn down because the waiters in the restaurant couldn't hear what the customers were saying to them.

Mick

"Gents must wear a collar and tie at all times" the notice said in the foyer. It was something that Big Albert & Co loved to recite like a mantra to the crowd baying at the entrance.

One of Albert's team of bouncers was a man named Mick Walker, a one time singer with the Birmingham group 'The Redcaps'. Mick managed to be both tall, relatively slim and yet still have the profile and aura of a bouncer but always with the addition of a mischievous smirk ready to break out into a grin at any moment. Pranks and humour were never far removed from Mick and in fact he divided his time between being bouncer and stand-up comic, as well as often indulging his musical bent by joining the groups in impromptu performances.

One evening, while the group were on break, the taped music suddenly stopped and Mick appeared from the rear of the small stage. The customers gasped. So did we. He was wearing nothing but socks and underpants and the collar of a shirt from which hung a somewhat poorly knotted tie. He strode up to the microphone:

"Ehem... Ladies And Gentlemen. Your Attention Please. May I remind you that Gents MUST wear a collar and tie at all times. If anyone in the club is *not* properly dressed they will be asked to leave. Thank you for your co-operation." Like a model on the catwalk, Mick whirled around and exited the platform with excessive feminine wobbles of his backside while we all roared with laughter and the girls in front of the stage covered their mouths and gawped wide-eyed at his spindly white legs.

Trial Flight

It was in 1973 that my womanising finally reached a natural point of crisis. For years I had cruised blithely upon an ocean of love affairs and uncommitted liaisons. The loving was followed by the leaving and that was about the only discernible order in my history of relationships. Somewhere I wanted to have a stable partnership but the idea of commitment horrified me. I hated the idea of marriage – as far as I was concerned that was the pits.

Disaster came at me in the form of a lover who I revered, adored and depended upon. Yes, for her I ripped songs from my heart and wove yarns for her into melodies galore. I worshipped the ground beneath her while the ground beneath me slowly gave way as she let me down flat. It upset me so much that I completely lost the plot. I hit the bottom with a wallop and sank into a mire of *morosity* (if there is such a thing). What made it worse was the feeling that somewhere she had only rendered unto me that which I had so often visited upon others.

I fell off the bottom rung of my ladder of life and began conspiring in earnest how I could end it all. I finally decided that I would jump out of an aeroplane. Yes, that would show her, the rotter! It was in pursuit of this ugly plan that I went out to Halfpenny Green aerodrome, near Wolverhampton, one day. I had been there before and I knew where to find the parachute clubhouse. I made a bee-line for it, ready to go for the 'familiarisation flight' where my foul plan would swing into action. But the club door was locked with a note on it: 'CLOSED' it said. I had gone on the wrong day!

Not to be deterred, I walked over to the flying club. That had a sign outside advertising a 'Trial Flight' and I thought to myself: "That will do!"

The instructor and I strode out to the waiting Piper Cherokee aircraft. As we climbed inside I was horrified. He sat me on the left in the Captains seat (unknown to me, that's where a student always sits) but the entrance door was on the co-pilot's side – on the right. So the only way you can throw yourself out of one of those is to clamber over the instructor first! This prospect cast yet another infernal spanner into the works of my fiendish plan.

As we sailed through the sky that day and I looked down nervously at the Shropshire earth below I realised something about me that had nothing to do with being scared of the long drop down. I recognised the evil thing that had carried me to the airport that day. I realised I had it all wrong. I didn't want to jump out of this aeroplane or out of life. I wanted to master this thing and master life.

It's funny how disaster can wind up being a creative force. It was really that miserable beginning that caused me to take up a Private Pilot's Licence course. On my wages from the 'Rum Runner', I realised I could just about afford it – if I was frugal. I promised myself I would not buy a drink for six months. And that's what I did. From September 1973 for the next six months, I never bought a single drink at the 'Rum Runner'. I was husbanding every penny toward my flying training course at Birmingham Airport. On 14 March 1974 I passed the final flight test and became the proud owner of a Private Pilot's Licence. After that I used to harvest passengers from the stream of revellers at the 'Rum Runner' and take anybody who wanted to go flying on trips to airfields around England.

Flying soon became the brightest star in my firmament, eclipsing music and girls and every other point of luminescence. I loved it. Whereas I always felt a bit of a flop at music, not being a natural virtuoso to put it mildly, with flying I swam through the course with ease. Learning all that stuff was pure joy for me and I found I had a natural aptitude for learning about the concepts it involved.

Yes!

It was an era where I was saying "yes" to everything. So for example when a friend named Kim Holmes came into the 'Rum Runner' one night and sidled up to Tony Clarkin and me at the bar, musing aloud that he needed a carpenter to build his new recording studio on Bristol Street – *and did we happen to know anybody who did that sort of thing?* – I immediately said: "YES, – we can do it!"

"Excuse me – Who is this WE you were referring to?" Tony asked as soon as Kim was out of earshot.

"You and me of course" I said, "we can build it for him. You're good at building things and if you tell me what to do, I can help."

Tony and I built 'Nest' studios for Kim. It took us about three months beginning in October 1973. We would play the 'Rum' in the evenings and work every day building 'Nest'. One day a week I would slink off taking my flying lesson. When the studio was finally complete, we used it to record many songs. Later in the 70s I recorded there with Jim Cleary, and also did the demo for my song 'Princeton' amongst others.

Tony

One day in October 1974, while 'Magnum' were at the 'Rum Runner', Tony Clarkin announced to us that he had decided to leave the group.

"It's time I got a proper job" he said, as we stared at him dumbfounded.

After the shock had subsided, we talked it out and decided on Pete Oliver as his replacement. Pete was a well respected guitarist who ran the local music shop in town. He could play country picking stuff better than anyone around and loved anything and everything that the Eagles recorded. Magnum's repertoire promptly began to include country music and the songs of the Eagles. But it only seemed like a few weeks before Tony appeared in the club one night and told us how he had realised he wasn't cut out for a proper job after all, and asked for his job back. I was the man elected to go and tell Pete the news!

I need not have worried. True to his easy going attitude, Pete was phlegmatic about it – he knew the group had been formed out of Tony's vision and understood. It was rock 'n' roll. Tony had got his vision back!

I was with 'Magnum' for two and a half years and for most of it we worked as the resident group at the Rum. It was the musical equivalent of a nine to five job, steady and secure and forgotten about as soon as you went home.

After the job at the 'Rum Runner' came to an end in June 1975, Magnum did some stints as a backing group on the cabaret circuit, providing the back line in turn for Eddie Holman, Mary White and Del Shannon, all of whom had at some point in time, been famous – in Del Shannon's case I think *mega-famous* is more appropriate. In 1975, 'Magnum' cut a couple of records which sank without a trace – 'Sweets for my Sweet,' an old 'Searchers' hit from the 60's that we resuscitated with a manic beat courtesy of Kex, and a song I wrote called 'Baby I Need' which was never released. I don't remember who the baby was, but my need at the time was for a change from strumming bass guitar as loud as possible. I didn't really feel in my heart that *Heavy Metal* was for me and at the end of 1975, I left 'Magnum'.

Tony Clarkin went on as the writer and leader of Magnum – a group devoted to his beloved heavy metal music. He became skilled in producing and arranging songs and in 1980, he played on my song 'Ria' which ended up on the 'Earth Rise' album. He figured that song out one day in the house I was looking after for Geoff Turton in Northfield. We recorded it on 8-Track and years later the playing and singing was lifted onto a 24 track, and drums and backing vocals woven around what Tony and I had laid down back in Birmingham.[3]

A little bit of knowledge

In 1977, I was living with Sheila, in her house. Sheila worked, I didn't. I stayed at home composing songs and working on projects, a bohemian freeloader full of promises but without the wherewithal.

I was on the dole but they wouldn't pay me anything. Every week I went to the seedy office at Sheldon and sat in front of the grill with my complaint of poverty, and every week a girl stared dispassionately back at me and intoned the same words:

"I'm sorry Mr. Morgan but you are not eligible for unemployment benefit because your girl friend is working."

In desperation I looked up the phone number for the Claimants' Union. I telephoned and made an appointment. Sheila and I drove over to the address in Balsall Heath. We expected an office but the address was a terraced house. A big black lady opened the door holding a tea-towel in one hand:

"Yes, you got de right place, dis is de Claimants Union – come in!". We were ushered into what was obviously her sitting room. She excused herself and went into the kitchen to finish up what she was doing and then came back wiping her hands on a towel and sat down:

"Now, tell me de nature of de problem?"

I told her about my weekly visits to the Sheldon benefits office and my unsuccessful pleas for help, and suddenly she exploded. Standing up she began to speak forcefully:

"You listen to me. You go back there again, and you ask dem to show you 'where is the clause in de social security charter where it sez de woman must keep de man!' – The Social Security charter sez de man must keep de woman but nowhere sez de woman must keep de man! You sit there and you don't leave de office until dey tell you where it sez this. – You promise me, you will sit until dey say where!"

She repeated herself in her strong Jamaican accent and made me promise that I would sit in the Social Security Office until they answered the riddle she had set.

The young girl behind the grill said the same as before:

"Sorry Mr. Morgan we cannot pay you anything because your girl friend is employed."

I repeated the phrase as near exact as I could remember it:

"Please would you show me the clause in the Social Security charter where it says that a woman must keep a man." The girl looked stunned. She stared at me silently for a few seconds and then got up.

"Hold on please."

She disappeared behind the upright screen dividing the beggars from the kings, no doubt to ask the majesties beyond what manner of words, or what composure of clause or regulation could be summoned to dispel me most rapidly from her concern and her desk window. I looked around at the exhortations stuck upon the furnishings and walls: 'Don't forget you can claim for this or that benefit if you or your partner are this or that....' The notices to the vagrant class to which I belonged, instructing all in what manner it was fitting to approach the throne. The begging bowls must be of certain dimensions and be proffered at the correct time, but the tinkle of cash was assured by royal edict.

Suddenly she called me:

"Mr. Morgan?" I looked up, her head was craned over the divider:

"Your case has been re-assessed and you will be getting £52 per week, back dated to when you signed on. Okay?"

"Er..Thank you" I said, but she had already slunk back behind the divider.

I've heard it said that a little bit of knowledge is a dangerous thing, but I know from experience that sometimes a little bit of the right information can go a long way, sometimes it can save the day. The Claimants Union didn't look like much, but that Caribbean lady with the tea towel sure knew her stuff.

A New World

It was one of those drunken nights at Frank Skarth-Haley's place in Erdington in 1978. Yes, Frank[4], mad as a hatter and twice as sweet, plied me with flatteries and scotch and I was a willing participant in the empire of dreams that he ruled. Frank was some kind of recording executive with a spread of wisdom that began as tittle-tattle and grew to genius status as I viewed his world from the bottom of my whiskey glass. It was at Frank's that I first heard Jeff. I mean really heard what he'd been doing. I was just blown away. Frank put on an ELO record and against a liquid haze I sat listening to the opening track: I remember the feeling of complete awe and at the same time, I was curiously inspired. The song was so full of fun. It was a tonic of joy and positivity:

They say some days you gotta win,
they say some days you gotta lose.
But baby I got news for you,
you're losing all the while you never win'.

It was in your face. In the words and the tune. It was pointing up, looking up, taking up. Anyway, it took me up. And I realised that Jeff had pushed on a door and gone on further than I ever had.

Nothing Says

The first time you hear a great song can often be a moment frozen forever in time. It is also the instant you really know how good the song is. That's the thing about the first time, it's a point of ultimate revelation: The time you know that there is nothing so beautiful as that you have seen, and long to see again.

There are many Beatle's songs, which stopped me in my tracks when I first heard them. 'Eleanor Rigby' is one; I first heard it when I was driving through the centre of Birmingham in my Jag. I pulled over, parked up and listened to it, mesmerised. To me it was just enchanting and beautiful. Long after it had finished I was still transfixed in a stupor, just wishing to hear it again: 'All the lonely people, where do they all belong?'

Many years later, in 1976, another great song came to visit upon me not from the speaker of a car radio but from the proverbial *horse's mouth* as it were, sung by its creator and custodian, a rotund bearded Irishman named Jim Cleary. I was visiting a pub in Moseley village, Birmingham and Jim was one of a three-piece group playing to the packed room.

One of the songs they performed that night was 'Nothing Says' and instantly, like 'Eleanor Rigby,' it was a slice of music I just wanted to hear again and again. It glowed with a timeless circular message that came through loud and clear – *Nothing says goodbye like a tear* – but the musical pirouettes it danced around to transport that message was, upon first hearing, a pure enigma to me. Jim had a way of honing chords that confounded any rules of music I knew about. After meeting him and hearing more of his songs, I soon discovered that 'Nothing Says' was not a fluke or a one-off, but just one of a whole series of devastatingly original songs by Jim. I was instantly jealous and conspired to be in a group with him, maybe to discover where he kept his vial of secret tunesmith unction and yes, to steal a bit of it if I could.

I fast became privy to Jim's Irish proclivity for Guinness – with or without a whiskey chaser, depending on the position of the sun over the yardarm – and for a while I thought maybe the secret unction was in that, but of course it wasn't. It was in places I could never reach – growing up in the streets of Dublin, migrating with mom and everything you can carry onto the Holyhead Ferry and the promise of prosperity in Birmingham, and finally the fine halls and finer verbiage of the University of Birmingham to buff and polish the rich tapestry that the university of life had already given him.

I was to spend many happy hours in the company of Jim's effervescent banter: the whiff of the Blarney mixed as it was and still is, with his studied Etonesque vocabulary imbibed from his University days.

We became pals and before too long I had teamed up with him as 'Morgan Cleary', first as a duo and later, as a trio with the addition of lead guitarist Bob Daffurn. During 1976 we were playing local folk clubs and pub sets in and around Birmingham.

Then in the autumn of '76 Richard Tandy breezed back into Birmingham from his globetrotting travels with ELO. He called me to say that he was able to get studio time to record my songs with him producing, and did I want to make an album?…

"Wow Rich – Yes! But er…" Richard had never heard of Jim Cleary and was a little taken aback when I tentatively proposed the album be of Jim and me instead of just me, but after hearing Jim's songs (I think we sang them together in the sitting room of his Moseley flat), Richard was soon sold on the idea. Studio dates were booked at DeLane Lea studios in Wembley, North London, and during November and December of 1976 we spent seventeen days recording twelve tracks for an album produced by Richard Tandy for Jet Records (Don Arden's label, made recently rich by ELO's successes).

Under Richard's aegis, we were swept up to unheard-of levels of swish: we were chaperoned to London in a big Ford car driven by Upsy; booked into a proper hotel instead of one of those seedy Bayswater bed and breakfast places with beds you were reticent to lie on and toilets you were scared to sit on. And the place itself – DeLane Lea – this was not built like an adjunct to somebody's shed as we were used to – No, it was a proper recording studio, the best I had ever seen and one I believe that ELO had previously used. At any rate, I remember Don Arden's office had an account with them and picked up the tab (or do I remember it because they *didn't* pick up the tab? It's one or the other…)

Yes it was a side of the music biz where the grass was definitely greener and Richard was eager to show it to us and to broaden our vista a little toward the glad hand of fortune that had broadened his so generously. There, with a proper sound engineer, we laid our souls bare before proper microphones wearing proper stereo headphones. No expense was spared. If josticks and camel sauce be ordered along with fish and chips then God forbid the roadie to come back without it as specified. Steve Wheate came down to help us with drums and Jim Cleary entertained us magnificently with his Irish caricatures, quips and beer cans, and when they ran out and Jim fell spark asleep one night, we bound him from head to toe in gaffer tape as he lay on the studio couch and then denied all knowledge of it when he woke up snorting like a polar bear in his straight-jacket truss several hours later.

But all that glitters is not necessarily the source of the Nile and the end of the story is that our finished album was never released. It languished somewhere in the vaults of Jet Records, my six songs and Jim's six – for a short while the toast of the town, but thereafter condemned to be orphans of unknown whereabouts.

The end of the recording sessions, marked also the beginning of the end of the Morgan Cleary group.

Show business is both a 'show' and a 'business' and in it you oscillate between the two. So our show ended and our business began with talk of deals flowing between London and Birmingham like pieces of paper blowing on the wind. Somewhere beneath the paperwork and ever more mystical promises of Jet Records, our little ship capsized and slowly sank along with our dreams of hit albums, or even released albums. At any rate Morgan Cleary didn't last too long after DeLane Lea.

And when it was finally ended it was all I could do to get the disappointment out of my system and roll it all up into a song called 'Princeton' (and I suppose in some weird way the University town signified a place of discovery, like we had stumbled upon the secret of how to build a new particle accelerator or something. But really I was just thinking of Jim's wonderful music and Irish prose, his lepricorns and space ships and the planets they took us to, the sheer magic of it all. Princeton was the town of the Prince, and Jim was the Prince). Anyway 'Princeton' was my message to the cosmos, a swan song in memory of our little group which I loved dearer than any woman.

But back to Jim's song... *Nothing says goodbye like a tear and nothing says hello like a smile.*

Yes it was burnt into the oxide at DeLane Lea but I have to say it never quite recaptured that magic I had first heard in Moseley, never quite made it back to the summit, and that crystal-untouched snow. For me, somehow the picture was overlaid with the slushy footprints of our exertions. But like an inconsolable lover, the song would not let me go and years later I had yet another go at it. In 2001 with Jim's permission, I did a version of it and released it on my 'Reel Two' CD.

Full Circle

The seventies had opened for me with Lou Reizner coming up to Birmingham and signing me up as a songwriter and recording artist. But by 1972 I was in dispute with him about my publishing agreement. Although Lou had let me go as a recording artist, he resolutely refused to let me go from the song writing deal. He suggested I speak with his lawyer in New York, one Marty Machat. Marty was a small guy with a big presence. I've heard that Hitler was the same. Anyway Marty *bless him*, told me that my publishing contract could be terminated no problem, providing that I sign over to Lou's publishing company – I think it was thirty three and a third per cent – of all future song writing income.

"What?" I recoiled, but Marty was way ahead of me in cool:

"Rod Stewart can do it. Why can't you?" was his parting shot and I had nothing to follow that.

I had known Lou Reizner as a paragon of virtue in the business of self-care. He was for sure a picture of health, a pin-up for a body builder mag, had there been such a thing back then. It wasn't a surface affectation. I can describe Lou, without disrespect, as a complete health nut. Of course unlike me, he didn't smoke or drink alcohol. In fact he would only drink bottled water shipped in from France. He ate all the *right* kinds of foods – strange stuff that I had never heard of. Nutty things floating in strange sauces, cardboard wheaty flakes that stuck to the roof of your mouth, to be washed down with the inerrant juices of some obscure, but healthy vine. (Dinner time at Lou's place had been a pinnacle of torture for me, there were no beans on toast or chip butties to be had there!).

So when Steve Wheate brought me the newspaper cutting reporting that Lou Reizner had died in June 1977, aged just 44, after a protracted illness, I found it deeply shocking. I knew so well the priority he had set on things that should have guaranteed his eminent longevity.

It was about a year after Lou died that 'Hiroshima' first became a massive seller in Germany. Lou's sub-publisher in Germany, Peter Kirsten, did not trust Marty Machat in New York and refused to send any publishing royalties to him before a deal was done to enable my share to be paid directly to me, something for which I am eternally grateful to him.

I never did get out of that publishing deal, eventually it just expired of old age. But the song 'Hiroshima', which Lou had spotted back in 1970 and made the flagship for the 'Wishful Thinking' album was to become a European hit not just once, but twice. Yet the Big Yank who had first nurtured it, never lived to partake of its success or the fulfilment of the fortune-tellers' declaration.

America 1970-71

Above: In the Coconut Groves, Florida (Foto by Stan Rosenblum).

Left: Warren Samet - 'The Bird', Right: Magic Bus Radio station in Miami - Amazingly their flyer pictures the front of a Midland Red bus, a common sight back in Birmingham.

The Looking Glass.1971-72
Flick, Randy, Paul and me pose for the group photo, Miami 1971.

Magnum 1973-75

MAGNUM

CBS's promotional flyer for the release of 'Sweets for my Sweet'. (28 Feb 1975).
From left: Tony Clarkin, 'Kex' – Kevin Gorin, Bob Catley and myself.

Photo Copyright CBS Records

Above Tony Clarkin of Magnum at Grimm Doo circa 1981.

Left with Jim Cleary

Ask for -
One More Day
by Morgan, on
Evolution EV.3
distributed by
RCA Records.

One More Day released March 1980.

FIVE – The TIME Tour

It was in June of 1981 when ELO were back in Birmingham after their jet-setting travels and during that summer Richard Tandy, Jeff and I would sit around drinking wine, strumming guitars and seeing how many Beatle songs we could remember between us. My love for John Lennon paid dividends – I knew quite a few of his bits.

Visiting Jeff's house one night, he played me ELO's new TIME album, and told me about the new tour in the pipeline. I have to admit I had always thought it was Jeff who called me up asking: "Would I like to come and sing with his group?", but checking my diaries, in fact I see it was me who called him up in late July and asked,

"Is there anything I can do to help out on the tour ..?"

This was a coded way of saying: "Help I need a job!"

"I don't know Dave. It's a nice idea but… the only thing is …"

"Yeah what?"

"You know being on tour is a sort-of… well, a pressured situation and …. it's just that I had a mate in the group before and we ended up falling out and now we're not mates anymore. I wouldn't want that to happen again."

I was relieved that was his reason and tried to assure him that it wouldn't be the case.

"Okay," he said, "let me think about it. We're practising tomorrow. Come over and we'll see how it sounds."

The exhaust promptly fell off my car the next morning as I set out for the rehearsal at Jeff's place. I arrived late, covered in oil...

Within two days the new line-up for the 'TIME' tour was revealed: I was to play guitar, help with the singing and provide some extra keyboard parts!

At that time, ELO comprised of four people – Jeff, Bev, Richard and Kelly. For the TIME tour the stage line-up was to be augmented by three more to make a seven-piece concert band: Lou Clark, Mik Kaminski and me.

We rehearsed for three weeks at 'The Boggery' – a cricket pavilion in Solihull that also doubled as a Jasper Carrot's folk-club. Then on September 3rd we jetted off to Los Angeles, America – and the 'TIME' tour. I had flown across the Atlantic before but had always arrived feeling like I was a screwed up paper bag! This time we travelled First Class – upstairs at the front of a PanAm Jumbo Jet. I was amazed how fresh I felt when we arrived. Whether it was the wide seat, the legroom or the omnipresent pampering from the stewardesses, something made a big difference to that eight hour trip...

America

'Sex, drugs and rock 'n' roll' are the first things most people think of when you mention touring with a 'pop group', and that is usually what they want to hear – the 'dirt'. If that's what you are looking for, you need read no further, because I will have to disappoint. There was certainly sex, and there was certainly rock 'n' roll, but really the spirit of the slogan didn't belong. ELO were in a different part of the arena.

Ozzie Osbourne's wife Sharon, summed it up in a TV interview: Sharon, the daughter of ELO's one-time manager Don Arden, was recollecting how she once accompanied ELO on the road in the 70's and thought they were so boring and un-newsworthy that she herself threw a TV out of a hotel window in order to spice things up a bit! That really says it all.

What I remember most about being part of the Electric Light Orchestra is the tremendous good fun we had. Other groups may have behaved like Satyricon on the road, but ELO was more like Monty Python.

It was Kelly Groucutt, ELO's bass player, who inadvertently provided the first milestone of major comedy on the American tour.

It happened before we ever got before the crowds, while we were rehearsing in Los Angeles. The 'tour' almost ended right there and then, before it ever began.

We were in what is called a 'sound stage' – an enormous building used by the film studios.

The sound stage was really a cavernous, vast empty shed, with dimensions that had more in keeping with an assembly hall for Jumbo Jets than a rehearsal room. But it had an attribute of special interest to movie-makers which was that no light from outside was allowed to enter – not a single photon, not even with a pass signed by Cecil B. DeMille. Outside the door it was a blistering bright California day but inside, the only light was artificial. That meant it could be made completely dark, and I mean completely!

When all the lights were turned off, the only way you knew that you had not been suddenly stricken blind was that you could still see tiny glimmers, the pinpricks of red from simmering amplifiers and keyboards.

The stage set that we played on had been specially constructed for the TIME tour. We practised getting to our various positions in total darkness, helped by strategically positioned roadies with small pen torches, and of course, we rehearsed the music. While we played our set again and again, the lighting crew went over their moves, so that for example, the lights came up at the precise moment of the first downbeat, or went down at the instant the last note hit. We rehearsed until it was second nature to all of us. It was at the end of a song, when all the lights went off, that Kelly's circus career began...

The now familiar inky blackness descended like a blanket as the last chord died away.

Suddenly out of the silence there was an absurd raucous sound: 'KerBoingggg!' – I can only describe it as the noise you get when a piano hits the bottom of a lift shaft.

'What the...? someone said. Heart-stopping seconds went by, then all the lights went up again.

We looked around to see what on earth had happened...

Kelly was not on stage any more. He was lying on the concrete some eight feet below the level of the stage set... In the blackness he had tripped over a foldback speaker and fallen right off the front of the stage. His bass guitar, still switched on, had provided the death-knell 'Boingggg' that we all heard.

We looked down in horror. Kelly lay motionless as the road crew raced toward him.

"Don't touch him!" someone shouted, as if at the scene of a crime. We were sure he must be injured or worse... Kelly groaned and began to move.

"He's okay" someone said, meaning "he's still alive".

After a minute or so, he got shakily up to his feet, steadied by helping hands: "Are you all right?"

"Yeah" he said, with a reassuring smile as he looked up and realised the extent of his acrobatics.

We all breathed again. He was just bruised. It was amazing! That was a *big* drop!

But the sound of the chord he chimed in the blackness that day reverberated amongst us for long after. We descended into fits of laughter every time someone mentioned it.

Fred

It was in the same Los Angeles studio also that we were first introduced to Fred. – Fred was the robot that had been made especially for the 'TIME' tour, and he was to have an acrobatic career all of his own later on. As soon as he arrived, the crew went to work checking out his electronic responses and rehearsing his moves. Fred was controlled by radio from the side of the stage, and had lights inside the dome of his brain which glowed when he 'spoke'. Jeff borrowed my vocoder to record Fred's opening speech over the music introducing the show, a taped adaptation of 'Prologue' at the start of the 'TIME' album. When it was done, we all stood at the back of the giant studio to watch the first run…

The music swelled up from the blackout, while lasers began darting to and fro, like the uncertain chaos of creation. Frolicking coloured lights appeared, slowly dancing and rising with the music into brightness, and then in the cone of a spotlight Fred made his grand entrance from stage right. Like a Dalek Emperor he rolled with slow majesty to stage centre, turned and faced forward, and then 'spoke' the electronic message that Jeff had gifted to him, his 'brain' glowing as he did:

Just on the border of your waking mind, there lies another time, where darkness and light are one… Then, his word to humankind completed, Fred slowly retraced his steps off the stage as the lighting reverted back to total blackout, while the music reached up to a final crescendo. (That would be the cue for us all to get on stage and strike up with the first song, 'Twilight'.)

The whole thing was such a moving and powerful spectacle to me – I don't know if it was the shock of realising just how excellent this show was, or an unction of thankfulness that I could be part of such excellence, or just the sheer power of the display, but there in the darkness I had tears in my eyes. I was grateful the lights were turned off. Jeff navigated his way over to me by the light of his cigarette end and said,

"What do you think Dave?"

I just choked back: "Yeah that's good Jeff."

He must have thought I didn't like it very much. I couldn't speak. It was great.

Stardom

By September 1981, ELO – already a household name in America – had a new song about to break into the popular psyche – 'Hold on Tight'.

I was to quickly discover that being at that level of notoriety invited fresh problems: When you suddenly find yourself famous – as I did then – one of the first things you learn (apart from discovering how many relatives you have), is that you have also gained a cortège of followers – reporters and fans – who make it their life's business to 'stalk' you wherever you go. ELO had been this way before of course, and I benefited from their hard-won experience. Protection from unsolicited attentions was just a fiendish plot away….

It was back at the Boggery that I first became acquainted with their defensive systems. We were all presented with a list of fictitious names to choose from. I seem to recall that Jeff had a hand in making these up.

Anyway, it was a toss-up whether I was to be 'Bertram Stilt' or 'Wilf Stonker'. In the end I got to be Mr. Stilt and Mik Kaminski joined the Stonker family tree.

These spurious names, we were told, would be our only source of identification to hotels and airlines. Back in the cricket pavilion in rural England it had seemed like overkill...

"This is a bit over the top isn't it Jeff?" I said.

"You'll learn," he replied. And learn I did, as soon as we hit America.

Fan after all, is an abbreviation of the word *fanatic*!

Apart from protection, our aliases provided an ongoing font of hilarious moments.

At every check-in desk, at hotels or airports, we would gather around to listen with smiles while a clerk blandly called out these ridiculous names and handed us our room keys or tickets:

"Mr Stonker?"

"Yes, here!" Mik would cry back.

I remember a bell-boy coming into a posh hotel restaurant calling out loudly:

"Phone call for Mister Squash", and drummer Bev Bevan – alias Fenton Squash – duly responding. It was so ridiculous, and quintessent ELO, a group devoted to lightness and fun.

But the subterfuge worked. Our defensive shield remained largely intact. It needed to.

Chris

Chris, our bouncer, came with us everywhere. He looked like an A-team toughie who had repented and joined the Mormons. He always wore a tailored light grey suit and was our 'battleship-in-being' – largely ceremonial but with the potential to fire a broadside if needed. Chris walked with the gait of a sumo wrestler, but he spoke softly and his studied manner always exuded an aura of cultured, calm serenity. This only added to the impression of coiled menace. Jeff joked that he was only there to stop us all escaping back to England but often, we were glad to have Chris around.

One time we were in a bar-restaurant in New York. The entire group was sat together at a table in a booth when we were approached by a young man who recognised us. The lad sat down at one end of the table and started talking to Jeff. The patter had gone on for quite a while when Chris suddenly rose up and leaned right across the table from the other end of the booth and said 'excuse me' to the lad, while at the same time pulling a rolled up newspaper from under his arm. Chris opened out the newspaper, and inside was a walkman cassette player with the 'record' light glowing…

"Let me help you to the door" Chris said in his characteristic soft manner, as he escorted the young man away. He was always the perfect gentleman, and I never saw him threaten anyone. He didn't need to – All he had to do was stand up!

Tourists

Being on tour is like hitching a ride on a perpetual motion machine. It drives you, walks you, flies you, feeds you, – all in order to show you off faultless before your judges for an hour and a half's concert each night. Like a great shark that must always keep swimming or else it will sink and die, the machine you are on seems to be forever taking you from somewhere to somewhere else. It is an addictive but wearing beast to ride. It stops for a breath but you are so high on the thrill of its last gyration, you merely gawp wide-eyed as you stumble like a child going from one Disney ride to another.

Travelling around with a pop group was for me, like being with a party of tourists on the strangest of holidays. Along with the blood-pumping thrill of playing before thousands of screaming fans, the fact we were in a state of constant transportation brought its own excitements and terrors. It was a holiday with priceless perks, for like visitors from another world, we got to ride mostly in sumptuous style, one befitting the alien dignitaries we had become for the season.

In America, we had a four-engined airliner transporting us around for most of the tour. It was a lovely machine, a British-made Viscount – the first prop-jet airliner design in the world. Jeff dubbed it the 'Brown Beauty'. It was luxuriously appointed to seat about fifteen in a cabin capable of holding sixty passengers. Lou and Vic were the pilots and Christine was the stewardess.

One day she showed us her photograph on the front of Cosmopolitan magazine and told us how she used to have a career as a professional model. But Christine was always ready to prove she was not just a pretty face and at one stopover, Lou and Vic took her up on her challenge that 'she could do anything a man could do'.

She told me about it the next day:

"Do you know, they got me changing a wheel on the plane last night!" – Lou and Vic had sat drinking beers, laughingly issuing various instructions – how high to jack the plane up, which toolbox to find a spanner in – while she got covered in oil and grease changing the plane's wheel all on her own!

On the other side of the Atlantic, the 'Brown Beauty' was long gone and new, less salubrious winged horsemen were found for us to ride upon. One cold winter's night we rode to Edinburgh on a hired twenty-seater plane. After the show, when we came to return home, a white blanket of freezing fog had descended over Edinburgh. We climbed aboard and peered anxiously through frosted windows as the plane taxied at a snails pace from the terminal, groping its way through the fog to the take off point. Jeff, in fiendish playful mood, made an announcement welcoming us all aboard the 'Buddy Holly Express'. Bev pleaded with him to shut up but that just encouraged him more. He began singing out loud the song 'Raining in my Heart' with new custom lyrics ending in 'and it's freezing, and we're all gonna die'. It was deep, crisp and even that night: everything outside was unremitting white – the same colour as ELO's knuckles on that take-off.

In Europe we hired a French aeroplane replete with a stewardess who had all the personal attributes of nurse Diesel in the comedy film 'High Anxiety'. The plane did not move until she had double-checked that we were all strapped in and definitely not smoking, and we had paid due attention to her rendition of the safety drill for the 'enth time... and woe betide anyone caught unlatching a seat belt before the light was switched off!

I noticed on one of the trips that Jeff and Richard had become interested in the sound the engines would make as the aircraft taxied around airports. It was a sort of stroboscopic 'Doppler effect', as the propellers cut into the air. Jeff tried to tape it on a walkman, I think he wanted to use it as a sound effect on a record.

However the day that we came to leave Berlin, we all got to appreciate the Doppler effect full frontal: the aircraft was speeding along the runway, almost ready to take off, when a sudden 'thud' was followed by a bellow of that strobing prop sound, accompanied by an enormous sheet of flame down the one side of the plane – the side Jeff was sat on. The pilots slammed on the brakes, and then taxied round for another go.

Jeff was not amused:

"Tell 'em to forget it, I'm getting off" he said as I went forward to see what had gone wrong. Meanwhile, nurse Diesel was telling us all to be quiet and stay in our seats as there was nothing to worry about. The cockpit was crammed full of Frenchmen all chattering and consulting manuals and dials. They explained to me in broken English that an automatic feathering device had inadvertently cut in and shut down the engine. Eventually, after much argy-bargy, the crew managed to pacify Jeff about it and we had another uneventful take off apart from those white ELO knuckles once more gripping seat arms.

Wherever we landed, we had motorcades of limousines to carry us between airports and hotels, and then between hotels and gigs. In America they were usually the smart, black stretched Cadillac's (the sort that mob chiefs always seem to use in the movies).

In Sweden, we were met at the airport by a fleet of Mercedes waiting to take us to the hotel. I was ushered into the back of one all on my own. The convoy sped off into the wintry scene and quickly joined the motorway to Stockholm. I soon realised we were travelling extremely fast on the packed snow. I peered over at the speedometer and then slumped lower in my seat, it was reading 140 KpH. Not only that, we were tailgating right up the back of the car in front! I looked ahead and behind, all the cars were the same. The entire motorcade was snaking along like an express train, zooming across the frozen landscape as if linked together by invisible couplings. I was absolutely terrified.

Later I learned that ELO had hired the Limmo company which specialised in transporting around high-level diplomats. In order to forestall any possibility of terrorist interdiction, they had trained to drive like that, in convoy at the highest speed, bumper to bumper.

It gave me some inkling of what it is like being somebody like Henry Kissinger, forever being chaperoned under the threat of someone trying to shoot you or blow you up.

Roadies

Before my ELO days, being on 'the road' had meant carrying equipment, setting it up and fiddling with knobs, changing fuses, plugs and strings when they broke but at the level ELO were at, there was none of that. We had a veritable army of roadies who were experts at their job and looked after us royally. Along with the sound engineers, they made the job of playing with ELO a luxury: It was so much easier to perform your best when you had such professional help around.

Once we came to a concert hall early in an afternoon to rehearse a new idea. We entered the building and heard music playing:

"Boy that sounds good, wonder who it is?" .

"Maybe it's the support group..."

One of us sneaked over to the door to the auditorium and peeked through – It was our roadies having a jam on the equipment they had just set up!

The road crew were all American, hired with the rig as it were, but from Birmingham, Brian and Phil had rode with us to look after our personal needs.

Brian Jones was affectionately known as 'HQ', and he was indeed the man in charge of everything in our universe. His short, bespectacled frame, ever sported a knowing grin and a ready response to any inquiry. Whatever you needed, Brian would get it, or know how to get it. Phil Copestake, Brian's 'understudy', was amazing in a different way – years ago he was in Geoff Turton's backing group 'The Houston Treadmill'. When (in January 1970) Geoff offered me a job playing bass in the group, and I told him I didn't have a bass guitar, he said, "You can use Phil's – He's going to become the roadie!" Well I had known of people humping gear while aspiring to be musicians but never the other way around! But that was Phil, a salt-of-the-earth type, the obverse of the rock 'n' roll ego maniacs usually in evidence in and around groups.

While on the subject of roadies, let me tell you about the most famous roadie I ever knew: His name was John Downing but everyone knew him by the nickname 'Upsy'. I knew Upsy before the word 'roadie' ever entered the lexicon of language as a shorthand replacement for the title 'road manager'. Years ago, he lived just a half mile from me in Tile Cross, and once came marching up to me when I was fixing my car, and announced that he was going to be my manager! I remember being amazed at his cheek and optimism. Duly armed with tapes of my songs, Upsy went around pestering various artistes, before moving on to higher callings.

After being the flagship roadie for Birmingham groups 'The Move' and 'ELO', he went on to work for a host of high-level acts, the most notable being Jimmy Hendrix, who he worked with right up until he overdosed. Upsy became something of a legend in the rock 'n' roll fraternity of the time. If your group had Upsy as its roadie, it was a medallion of honour that would be bragged about as if Eric Clapton had been signed up to play guitar for you!

But he was to die in mysterious circumstances that will probably never be satisfactorily explained: There were no witnesses to tell how Upsy came to fall from the deck of a ferry into the North Sea one night in April 1987, but I digress…

Custard Pies

"Be on your guard tonight," Bev said, "the roadies usually have something up their sleeve for the last gig of a tour." It had become a tradition apparently, and the seventh of November 1981, was the last concert of the American tour, at Bloomington, Indiana.

Ever mindful of Bevs' warning, as I played that night I kept a watchful vigil on what the road crew were up to, especially during the bits when the lights were low...but nothing happened. I thought that maybe the idea of a dastardly prank has lost its shock value for them, or perhaps they planned to wreak some other kind of havoc, by spiking our drinks later, or something….?

As we were playing the last song, 'Roll Over Beethoven', I saw the unmistakable shape of roadies scurrying about, carrying something, and I knew the hour of reckoning was drawing nigh. Sure enough I turned to see Brian Jones advancing up the steps of my rostrum clutching a paper plate, which had on it a white gooey mass. I danced around the plinth with him for few seconds while he grinned at me, but I had nowhere to go. I couldn't even lift a finger to protect myself – I had my hands full playing the guitar – when he finally let me have it in the face. It was a sort of cross between custard soufflé and shaving cream and it obscured my view of everything for a moment, until I could blow if off my eyes. Looking around I could see Bev was equally afflicted and Lou Clark and Mik Kaminski were about to get theirs.

Then I looked down at the rest below. Kelly was at the front of the stage, oblivious to what was happening behind him. He stood with one foot on a foldback speaker, legs set wide apart, the neck of his bass guitar pointed into the air triumphantly. Half of ELO had by now turned into Christmas decorations and looked like frostbitten Eskimos, but Kelly couldn't see. The crowd at his feet beamed, and as Brian Jones approached him from behind across the big stage, their beams became beamier and they gagged and screamed in ecstatic delight. All eyes in the University of Indiana were focussed on one person. And he was loving it, his guitar neck rose higher, the crowd roared louder…

Brian Jones stood right behind him barely a foot away, holding his paper plate like a waiter in a period play. He was a star in his own right for a full ten seconds. Finally he tapped Kelly on the shoulder and, as he turned his head, let him have it, full frontal.

It was the quickest fall from grace I ever saw.

Red Wine and Suicide

The American, and then the European tour, sped by in a blur of ritual activity:

Limmo from Airport to hotel; – Limmo to gig, play;

Limmo back to hotel, after-gig booze-up, sleep-breakfast; – Limmo to airport, fly to next town.

And so on it went, for 37 shows in America and then 32 in Europe.

Endless fun and jokes made it a voyage of delight for me.

I spent most every night after a concert, in Richard's hotel room where, along with Jeff, I would attend the 'red wine club'. It was a select fellowship largely because the rest of ELO were off doing the sorts of things that people in groups do, and rarely bothered to drop in. The red wine club was a dependable haven of zany banter and untold merriments: Songs of infinite silliness would be composed and then forgotten amidst gales of laughter. Once in a rare interlude of taste and seriousness we tried to perform a rendition of Jim Cleary's song 'Modeste the minor poet'. Even Richard couldn't figure out its unique chords, and we ended up impulsively calling Jim back in England, as if it were a matter of urgent national importance. In the middle of the night, he tried to explain over the phone which finger went where on the strings, but we never did work it out.[5]

Fred, our loyal robot, performed faithfully for nearly all of the 69 shows. I say nearly all, because one night in Europe, Fred tried to end it all after receiving a welter of bad vibes that befuddled his overworked brain. As well as introducing the show Fred always came on for the last number of the night. He would join Mik Kaminski at centre stage in a wild dance during the long solo in 'Roll over Beethoven'. Mik and Fred would circle each other, as if mimicking each other's gyrations in a sparring match that looked like a Ukrainian dance version of 'Star Wars'.

Members of the road crew operated Fred from a console hidden behind the house speakers on my side of the stage. That night from my rostrum overlooking them, I could see that something had gone horribly wrong. A gaggle of roadies were stood gesticulating at Fred's spasticated movements, and like passengers in the back seat of a car without a steering wheel, they were shouting instructions to the driver struggling at the controls.

But Fred was getting signals from elsewhere… Afterwards, we accused the police. But whether it was them, or signals from outer space, Fred was moved to a fit of spontaneous jerks that suddenly caused him in a moment of apparent digital revelation, to stop and face the audience, and then traverse the entire stage area in one orgasmic bound of energy that shot him right off the front and onto foldback speakers some feet below. The crowd loved it. The roadies were horrified. Like fire crew homing on a downed aircraft, they all rushed to his assistance. While the music played on, they carried Fred off feet first, his little toes turned up to the roof lights. He was seriously in need of surgery.

But although he had a fractured head, our ever resourceful road crew team had him back on his feet again for the next show, albeit with several windings of gaffer tape over the cracks in his Plexiglas cranium.

The TIME tour made its final curtain call at Munich on 5 March 1982.

We flew back home to Birmingham the next day. I think all of us were aware that an era had ended.

TIME TOUR 1981-82

On the Top of the World 1:

Riding the 'Brown Beauty' - our executive Viscount - to the next gig. At left is Kelly, standing is Neil Quateman (one of the management team), at right is Richard and behind him, Pam talks to our minder, Chris Arnstein. The Brown Beauty was used from 10 October until the end of the tour, 7 November 1981.

On the Top of the World 2: Pam and I catching the view from the top of the World Trade Center, New York, October 1981.

Cincinnati 6 November 1981 On the airport tarmac. Hal Shevers (left) meets Lou and Vic, the pilots of ELO's 'Brown Beauty' (in the background).

Stockholm, 6 Feb 1982 Backstage after the show, ELO are visited by Anni-Frid Lyngstad - 'Frida' - of ABBA (second from right).

The Rat Club, December 1981. An outhouse at Jeff's home that was once a barn is pressed into service as a practise room. Inside it is a cramped, dark and rather seedy affair with all the ambience of a Beirut night club. So Jeff called it the Rat Club. On the right is roaddie Brian Jones, affectionately known as 'HQ'.

Christmas 1981. Roy Wood giving the thumbs up at a party in Jeff's house.

European tour 1982 Kelly and Jeff are in the spotlight at a German concert. In the foreground is the domed head of Fred, the suicidal robot.

SIX – All You Need is Cash!

Earth Rise

It was just a photograph in a magazine.

They were orbiting the moon in the LEM – the 'Lunar Expedition Module' – and as they swung around its 'dark' side, the earth came into view above the moon's horizon – a semi-circle of blazing colour emerging out of the lifeless undulating blanket of the moon's grey surface beneath them.

I looked at the photograph and its enigmatic inscription: 'Earth Rise'. I asked myself: "Earth rise or earthrise – is that one word or two??" It was a photograph of a view that no human being had ever seen before, and no words had ever been set to describe it. 'What a lovely expression' I thought, 'Earth Rise' – and immediately a song percolated into my thoughts.

It was in 1969 when man first stepped out of a spaceship and stood on the Moon. Everyone on planet Earth was looking up at the sky and everyone worshipped at the temple of NASA, the keeper of the Holy Grail, a future of unbridled excellence, the dream of the entire planet.

The moment I saw the picture I was there in that LEM, and I knew that although I was a born-again, evangelical, NASA-believing pragmatist, in that moment I was nothing but one solitary, lonely, human being.

The song just wafted up from the picture. Another song, and then another just fell off the back of the first one forming a medley, and before long I had a suite of music which I recorded on my old B&O (Bang & Olufsen) recorder. I had written nearly half of what was to become, years later, the album 'Earth Rise'.

Richard was to be the prime mover in getting 'Earth Rise' into production. He heard those original 'Earth Rise' tracks and fell in love with the idea. Later I re-recorded some of the tracks on a Teac 4-Track recorder in the front room of Sheila's house in Yardley and some of those early demos made it onto the final record – but only after we had tried unsuccessfully to re-record them.

Between ELO tour dates in the 70's Richard and I would meet up and he would often mention 'Earth Rise' as an album project he would like to record one day. But it wasn't until after the TIME tour of 1981 that an opportunity came up to do that.

In Los Angeles, Richard's friend Debbie Spencer Rose, had introduced the 'Earth Rise' demo tapes to a British entrepreneur named Brian Leahy. One thing led to another and by 1982 a deal was struck and we began recording at Ridge Farm Studios, a sumptuous country residence in Sussex, kitted out as a hotel and studio replete with a swimming pool and all the trimmings of fame.

Yes, 'Earth Rise' took a long time to come to completion. It was quite an epic project and without Richard's dedication it would never have made it.

Richard Tandy was in ELO from the very beginning back in 1972. He started off playing guitar, and even singing, but soon transferred onto piano. Soon the term 'piano player' was to be superseded by 'keyboard player' as synthesisers, melotrons, and later, vocoders, became the instruments shaping the musical fashions of the day.

I don't think there was a gig on the TIME tour where Richard travelled with us from the hotel to the concert. He was always there a couple of hours earlier than us and we would find him sat alone in a back-stage room practising away at a piano. It became part of the roadies drill to set up a spare Wurlitzer for Richard in a changing room. From when I first knew him he was always a man of extraordinary patience and dedication.

In my limited knowledge of ELO making records, he never left Jeff's side while the business of producing music was going on. You might think 'so what' but I have to tell you that making a record can often be a very boring business to behold. Going over the same line for the 'enth time is no fun unless you're part of the creative loop doing it. If you are a spectator on the outside looking in, it can be pretty mind numbing. I was part of some ELO sessions in Holland (recording the album 'Secret Messages'), and I remember all of us spending most of the time playing table football rather than sit in the studio. All except Richard that is. Richard never budged from his seat at the studio mixing desk, where he was the omnipresent sounding board for Jeff as he wove his masterpieces.

He was just the same with me when we recorded Earth Rise, a witness to every detail of the project, and every note that was played. He only missed one session of recording: One day, he had to keep an important appointment in London. It was agreed that I would get on and tidy up 'Princeton', a song already virtually complete and *in the can* as it were. (Princeton had been recorded some years before and Brian Leahy had purchased the tapes for the Earth Rise project). Richard arrived late that evening to listen to the mix that producer Steve Lipson and I had worked on.

"Hmm" he said pensively, "I feel I have to do something on it, but I don't want to spoil it."

Steve and I proffered some suggestions for overdubbing various things, but he just shook his head darkly. Eventually he said:

"How about if you turn the mic on and just record me breathing on it!"

"Okay" said Steve, always ready for the zaniest ideas.

We were about to do just that when he got the inspiration to play a subtle guitar part over the long fade at the end. I can still hear it way back in the mix, Richard breathing on 'Princeton'.

That's what having Richard around was like. No matter if he played or not, he breathed on everything and that made the difference. You couldn't have Richard around and not be influenced by his restrained gentleness and good musical taste. As far as I am concerned, Richard's presence in a recording studio was always a beneficial thing, at the very least it was keeping me safe from my own hair-brained ideas! Thinking about it, I've come to the conclusion that there ought to be a credit invented for it – a credit for just 'being there': Yes, the text on the sleeve of 'Earth Rise' should have this added to it: 'Presence: Richard Tandy'.

There are many songs on Earth Rise that I can't listen to without being immediately transported to the antics that went on while we were recording them, and the canvas of rich suburbia that they were painted against.

Our engineer-cum-producer Steve Lipson looked like a cross between Rasputin and the pictures of Jesus you see in children's books. He looked like that all the more first thing in the morning when he would often appear silently and suddenly along some dimly-lit corridor, draped in a grey flannel dressing gown that resolved a short distance above scantily shod feet, his unruly beard locked in a coalition of anarchy with his uncombed hair. To see Steve before breakfast was to have a vision of the second coming. Steve was a revolutionary in any and every way, a subversive to anything you might treasure as normality.

One morning Richard was late finishing breakfast and I left him and went on ahead to the studio. I walked in the control room to find Steve down on his knees beside the effects rack. He was holding up a microphone to his nostrils and every now and then, he would make a rather aggressive sniffling sound.

I watched in quizzical awe as he made several samples of this nasal affectation until, satisfied he had achieved the right level of retch, he got up smiling and strode over to the desk. After making some adjustments, he played me the track with this snort inserted in it to form part of the beat. It was really quite magic – it fitted great. I can still hear Steve's nose every time I play the song 'Spaceship Earth'.

Like on nearly all my records, I sang most of the vocal parts on Earth Rise, building the block harmony pieces bit by bit by successively singing each part. It's not quite as laborious as it sounds. Once you know what you are aiming at, it can be a quick, straightforward process. One of the songs had a bit where the words: 'Morning's come' heralded the start of a new verse in three-part harmony. I was in the middle of doing the singing when Richard cut in to tell me a vision that had just crossed his mind – It was of a Roman Emperor appearing on a balcony, one arm raised imperiously, greeting the gathered crowd below with the words: "Morning *scum*." That was it. We all fell about laughing. From then on every time we got to that part of the song I just fell apart. It cost us a lot of money in studio time to record that one line in 'Pictures in my Pillow'.

We worked on Earth Rise throughout the summer of 1983, mostly at Ridge Farm in Sussex but also at other state-of-the-art studios in and around London. As well as the almost-complete 'Princeton', the song 'Ria' was lifted off my eight track recorder and grafted onto 24 track studio tape, so that everything except the singing and Tony Clarkin's guitar parts could be re-done. Right at the very end of the project we met Martin Smith, and he actually contributed a guitar part on the closing track of 'Earth Rise'.

Finally, the album was finished. We climbed out of the driving seat and became passengers in the back while deals and rumours of deals passed by like signs pointing to heaven. Eventually the signs became more infrequent and by early 1984, they had disappeared altogether. In the end, the Earth Rise album was never to get the major label release that Richard and I had hoped for, and was taken up by small independent labels only. Such is rock 'n' roll!

Paradise Garden

Martin Smith had grown up in the badlands of North London and then spent years working as a staff producer for Jerry Bron of Bronze Records. Somewhere along the line he had learned how to spot the potential of a good song in amongst a pile of pithy demos and crucially had gleaned a constitution able to take on board the thankless task of lovingly drawing out that promise, through long hours of careful coaching.

Martin always used to tell me that "the three most important things about a hit song are: number one, the song, number two, the producer and lastly, the singer."

Well I had the songs but many of them were no more than wayward, unruly children that had previously defied all attempts to mould them into fine upstanding citizens. Until they met Martin Smith, that is. Through sheer hard slog he figured out how to trap them, and then to tame them. He combed their hair, put a collar and tie on, gave them some discipline and made them presentable, many for the first time.

But there was one song that was so dysfunctional, so unkempt and out of control, it was like a junkie with a speech defect – it couldn't tell you what was wrong, or how to make it feel better – you couldn't communicate with it – the chord structure was so weird and unwelcoming, the lyric was abrasive and the whole thing so far away from the pop song I longed to pen, I had long ago abandoned it:

"Get out of here you no good reprobate – you're no son of mine!"

I didn't even bother suggesting it until Martin had demonstrated, through incredible patience, his ability to break the will of my other rebellious kids, one by one.

'Paradise Garden' was, I believed, the best song I had ever written. I loved it and the fact that it was an irreparable tearaway only added to its mystique. I had burned myself out several times trying to record it, only to end up with a pile of useless gristle. I had worked on it with others: with Richard; with drummer Steve Wheate (himself a veritable genius at making a song work) but it never responded to treatment. I was convinced it was unrecoverable and un-doable!

But I loved this outcast no matter what grief it had caused me. I loved its strangeness most of all and was prepared to defend it at all costs. Martin, as always set out first to discover how much of it I would really kill for, and how much was up for grabs. He took it apart bit by bit, to find out where the bottom line lay.

"Does it really need this bit?"

"YES!" I would scream back.

We negotiated like that – me fighting the rearguard action of a retreating army.

'Paradise Garden' was more of an odyssey than a song, droning on for about seven minutes in the original version. Although it was long, it had just two verses which were woven into a convoluted chord structure that defied natural order. It didn't have a chorus, nor an identifiable 'riff' – just lyrics, lots of them. A real loser! I could only compare it to a Bob Dylan song-monologue where, if you didn't like the words, you didn't like the song.

It took Martin about a week to capture it and cage it. We recorded it where we did everything, on the eight-track in the front room of my house. Then, at Martin's suggestion, we took a cache of the best songs we'd done and transferred them onto a 24-track professional format, and worked some more on them in a London studio. 'Paradise Garden' was one of them.

At the time, Richard Tandy was exiled in France for a year, escaping the British taxman, and so he hadn't contributed anything to the bulk of the tracks. He flew over from France for just a few days when we booked the London studio, enough time to add a couple of keyboard parts and, most importantly, to be present when the singing was done.

They say that 'work expands to fill the time available' and Martin and I had tentatively scheduled an entire afternoon to get the vocal on 'Paradise Garden'. Richard heard this and exploded:

"What do you mean all afternoon?" he thundered, "how long is the track – in minutes?"

"Er… about five minutes Rich" I said.

"Right, then that's how long it's gonna take" he shot back.

And that is exactly what happened. I got in front of the microphone, the engineer started the tape and five minutes later we had the vocal on 'Paradise Garden'. Richard was a bit edgy and impatient for those London sessions, anxious to get back to France and not compromise his tax status. He was only allowed a couple of days in England.

If I was the dysfunctional parent who constantly turned his kids out onto the street as they failed to meet their promise, Martin ran the boot camp that took them in and turned them around through a regime of hard discipline. It was shock treatment that worked.

We began working on the song 'Run Little Girl Run' in early 1985, and ended up some two plus years later with a song called 'Red Shift' (which has never been released). At the outset, Martin was working part-time as a hairdresser, and would drive up each week from Sussex to Birmingham to snatch two or three days recording time in my front room studio, called 'Grimm Doo'. The fact is, although he worked like a Trojan on my music, he never earned a bean from it. He never got any recompense for all the hours of dedication and commitment he put in to raising my kids at his boot camp. Not directly that is. But then a convergence of good fortune rose up and began to track Martin down, like a cruise missile on its run-in to the target...

It was late in 1985 when we worked on the 'Action' project. We recorded the final cut of 'Action' in the UB40's studio in a seedy part of Birmingham, and Martin played the lead guitar parts while Jeff Lynne, the producer, looked and listened.

He leaned over to me in a conspiratorial whisper:

"Martin's got a nice touch on the guitar. Do you think he could play bass?"

"Oh yes," I replied, knowing he could.

"Only, there might be a show coming up, and if it comes off, we'll need somebody to fill Kelly's position."

Martin became ELO's bass player for the 1986 shows....

Shortly afterwards he renewed a relationship that had lain dormant for many years with an uncle who was impressed with the fact his nephew had played at Wembley Stadium. This uncle had ownership in a very successful business and signed over to Martin a batch of shares. Just about one year later the business was subject to a take-over and those shares became worth big bucks. It was a real rags to riches story.

The next time Martin came to Birmingham it was in a sleek, low, brand new red Porsche 944.

Wembley Revisited

We had just come off stage at Austin, Texas, after the first show of the TIME tour in September 1981.

"Well done guys" said Bev, scanning around to address Lou, myself and Mik.

"Well of course, you've done it before" he added, looking at Mik, "but these guys haven't."

"Did you think they would bottle out?" someone asked.

Ever the diplomat he was (and he used to be in a group called the 'Diplomats' by the way), Bev answered: "Hmm well – you can never be one hundred percent sure how someone will react when they're confronted with a mass of screaming kids. But you guys did good. I was watching, you seemed to take it in your stride."

There was the hint in what he was saying that at some point in the past, someone had indeed 'bottled out' during an ELO concert. I didn't ask and I don't know. I was too concerned it might one day be me. Maybe I would notice all those people and suddenly decide to have a change of career...

But I have to say I didn't feel remotely like that at all – not then. Not at all until the day we were at Wembley Stadium, on Saturday afternoon, 5 July 1986.

We had played Wembley before – for six days in December 1981. But that was in the Arena, the indoor concert hall that seats about four thousand. Wembley Stadium was a different beast – the football pitch, together with the stands, were host to a crowd of sixty thousand people that day, by far the biggest crowd I had ever stood before.

We struck up with 'Twilight' as we had done so many times before... A short bit where Jeff sings the verse, and then it was time for me to move forward to help with harmonies on the chorus:

Shock, horror! For a full second my legs would not work! – I was rooted to the spot!

For one long instant, like a toad caught in the stare of a snake, I was paralysed before the avid gaze of thousands of eyes. I willed my feet one at a time to break their bond with the decking, and then issued mental threats to my legs, before they finally transported me over to the microphone at stage front. It was a shock – I didn't realise how nervous I was until I tried to move!

But as soon as the set was underway, I was fine.

If Jeff was nervous, it didn't show. There was just the customary fake panic before going on, when he whispered to me: "What comes after 'The visions dancing in my mind'?" (the first line to the first song of the show). It was totally normal for Jeff to forget words. It never seemed to faze him, he would just make some more up as he went along. Once I went to the trouble of writing out the words to John Lennon's 'Across the Universe' and pasting them to his foldback speaker so that he could sing the right lyrics for a change. It didn't make a blind bit of difference. That night as I listened with special attention, I heard yet another meandering prose vaguely based upon the original.

Before the mammoth congregation at Wembley, Jeff seemed uncommonly relaxed speaking to the audience between songs. It was something he usually avoided doing, but that afternoon he was mustard at it, talking to them naturally in his down-at-the-pub vernacular.

Murphy's Law

For Wembley and the German dates that followed, we had rehearsed in a seedy music bordello called the Nomis complex, in north London. It was built like a nuclear command bunker, with long concrete passageways flanked by oversize metal doors behind which the decibels pounded like tormented prisoners hammering to get out. Walking along the corridors into which this combined din exuded was like being privy to the cacophony of hell.

We were there for eight days, gathered together in one half of an enormous practise room.

One day a brand new string synthesiser arrived for Lou Clark to use. Helped by the roadies, Lou quickly ripped into the packaging, and then surrounded by Styrofoam and cardboard, set up the new instrument to begin investigating its potential. He was wide-eyed like a kid with a Christmas present.

Soon he had discovered a rich string ensemble sound and as if demonstrating it to a customer, began playing Beethoven's Ninth (the piece that introduces ELO's version of 'Roll over Beethoven'). Jeff's antenna was immediately raised and he rushed across to Lou:

"Hey, that sounds great! Why don't you play that on stage and then we can dump that tape we've been using. That sounds miles better."

"Oh no Jeff" said Lou, "I couldn't do that."

"Why not, you just did!"

"Yeah I know, I can play it *now*, but at night – on a show, you know after I've had a drink… I don't know.. I might mess it up…."

"Oh," said Jeff, understanding Lou's dilemma with a look of disappointment. It was quite a nifty piece to play… Jeff orbited around the room for awhile lost in deliberation and then wheeled back:

"But hang on Lou, hasn't that thing got a sequencer built into it?"

"Yeah, I think it has" said Lou, reaching for the handbook.

"Well in that case, you can record it. That will work. Then, all you'll have to do is play back the sequence and we can have that sound instead of the tape. That'll be much better!"

Lou spent the next three hours programming Beethoven's Ninth into the new string synthesiser using headphones while we were all practising other things. Finally he announced it was done and we all gathered around for the first rendition:

"Ready?" said Lou grinning. "Yeah" we all chorused back, "go for it!"

Lou theatrically presented a finger for us all to see and then pointing it at the keyboard, stabbed the play button. The music burst into life while he stood by, sporting a proud grin and pretending to play it. We partook of this swish performance and gave a warm round of applause.

"That's great Lou," said Jeff and it was quickly agreed, that is what we would use for the show instead of the taped introduction.

All went well until one night in Germany. Jeff announced we would be doing one more song: 'Roll over Beethoven'. The auditorium roared with applause and then the lights went down and the noise melted away to zero.

It was pitch black. An eery silence descended and absolutely nothing else happened. Just silence.....

Thousands of people normally make some noise even when they're not trying to, but that night they must have all been holding their breath because it was so quiet you could have heard a pin drop. Seconds ticked by while we all held our breath too. I could hear Jeff whisper in the blackness as clear as day: "Lou, hurry up will yer!" It was so quiet in that hall I think everybody heard it.

Nothing happened... just blackness and silence.

We stood cringing while that awful, evermore embarrassing silence grew and grew....

In the darkness I looked over in the direction of Lou's rostrum and saw tiny beams of pencil torches jostling about in a staccato hubbub of feverish activity, while I heard Jeff's whisper bark again, this time more frantic: "Come on Lou – What yer playing at?"

He might as well have shouted it.

Suddenly the music struck up. Phew! We were reprieved.

The crowd roared as if suddenly reincarnated. The lights went up and Hallelujah, Ludwig was away, galloping at full throttle. Brakes off, rotate – take-off!

"What on earth happened to you at the start of the last song?" Jeff asked the sixty-four thousand dollar question as we fell into the dressing room afterwards. Lou smiled the smile of the lampoon character who had trodden on a rake left lying in the garden while he rendered his plea of defence:

"I couldn't find the start button. It was too dark!" he said, "I had to get a roadie to come and shine his flashlight on the panel of the keyboard!"

We all doubled up in laughter.

It was the mythical Irishman Murphy who famously discovered one of the great immutable laws of life which is simply: 'If something can go wrong, it will go wrong'.

Needless to say, ELO invested in a little lamp to sit on top of Lou's keyboard after that.

Rod

Rod Stewart was top of the bill at Wembley, and for the short German tour that followed. Rod was, as advertised, the mega-star. I stood watching his performance one night in Germany. His theatrics and command of the audience was dazzling and there was a camaraderie between him and his group that told of their long association. They seemed to be pals as well as partners in a multi-million business.

I vaguely remember spending one drunken night in a bar with him and his group singing Irish-sounding shanties – one of his group carrying the lead while Rod and everyone else present chirped in with answer phrases and harmonies.

When it came time to fly back home from Germany, Rod was the mega-star in a more familiar way, the way that attracts notoriety. He was the Rod of the Daily Newsrag we all read about:

We were all seated on the British Airways Boeing with the door still open, wondering why were we waiting and what was going on. Maybe ten minutes ticked by and then out of the windows we saw the airport bus – the big articulated affair that could transport probably 150 souls at a time – it was trundling from the terminal with the unmistakable silhouette of one solitary occupant inside it. A dark shape. Someone wearing an enormous hat. The bus drew alongside. Rod and oversize hat skipped up the steps and was hastily directed into a first class seat near the front. The door closed, engines whirred, curtains were drawn, and promptly we departed for England.

The first show ELO played in 1986 was at the National Exhibition Centre. It was called 'Heartbeat' – a charity event to raise money for a children's hospice, and nearly every Birmingham artiste was represented. The Moody Blues were 'top of the bill' (ELO were next in line). The show was hosted by Jasper Carrot who introduced a multitude of Birmingham talent: Steve Gibbons, the Applejacks (the first Birmingham group to have a number one, reformed specially for the event), the Fortunes, Robert Plant, Roy Wood, and many more.

The ELO of 1986 was a different ELO from the one of four years before mainly because Martin had replaced Kelly on bass guitar. I suppose Bev must have eyed up Martin in the same way he had eyed up Lou Clark and me on the '81 tour. But Martin just looked like he had played big rock concerts all his life. I remember on the very first gig looking across to see him and Mik Kaminski prancing nonchalantly about the stage as if in some kind of aborigine line dance. Martin was just a complete professional.

"All You Need is Cash!"

It was late one sunny afternoon in July 1986 when we drove through the big iron gates into George Harrison's estate at Henley-on-Thames. The long driveway emptied out into a scene from Disney – a turreted mansion erupted out of the trees like an enchanted castle, replete with stone gargoyles that peered down from the parapets with questioning eyes:

Who's this lot coming in?

George's mate Jeff by the looks of it, with some of his crew from that group of his, that Eclectic Lice Ornaments lot.

"Cor, look at this place will yer…!" one of us whispered in the car below. There were four of us: Jeff, his personal road manager Phil Hatton, violinist Mik Kaminski and myself.

George was sat outside on a patio overlooking the grounds.

"Hello's" and nervous handshakes went all around before we sat down at the small picnic table bedecked with cans of beer.

He pointed to them, "Help yourself."

We supped beer while swiveling around in our chairs, to take it all in. George's castle hovered behind us while in front, a rolling landscaped garden; a playground of mother nature's best wares spread out around the castle and formed the 'estate' – more like a theme park than a back garden. George caught our eyes wide with wonder, and raising his beer can aloft as if to make a toast, announced with a wry smile: "All you need is Cash!" in playful parody of the song 'All you Need is Love' – and probably also, George Martin's book 'All you Need is Ears'.

He must have smelled the anxiety in the air and sensed the need for a joke. We all laughed and felt a little more at ease. Or maybe it was just me who was nervous. I remember, it was no different the first time….

We were playing at the National Exhibition Centre in Birmingham, some months before, in March 1986.

Jeff rushed in the dressing room and said breathlessly:

"Er, lads – He's here, he's just landed."

"Who?"

"George" said Jeff. "Yeah, he'll be coming down in just a minute. Try to make him feel at home will yer please. You know, just act normal, okay?"

"Yes Jeff" we all said with perfect timing for once. Thus reassured he disappeared to chaperone his friend, fresh from the helipad into the dark bowels of the NEC changing rooms.

Bass player Martin Smith looked down at his bare legs and hurriedly found his trousers, slithering into them at maximum speed. We all bumped into each other in the flurry of activity to get dressed so that we can concentrate fully on being normal. We've got to make George feel at home as Jeff has just instructed.

Enter George... Silence.

We are all lined up like toy soldiers, frozen to the spot, standing to attention in the cramped billet of the changing room. George smiles – "Hi" he says warmly but he might as well have screamed at us like a demented sergeant.

We make "Hello" and "Hi" – type noises while our bodies nod slightly as they spontaneously jerk in an involuntary bow before the great star. Jeff hovers behind his pal George Harrison glowering at us with his eyes: "I thought I told you lot to act normal!"

But what is normal about meeting a living legend? I mean what is a normal person supposed to do? Break wind or burp, do a silly dance, slap him each side of the cheeks like Morecambe and Wise?! You can't be 'normal' when you meet a Beatle because a Beatle is not a normal person. A Beatle is a star and a star is composed of different DNA to the likes of you and I, it's a well-known fact.

Somewhere between the slums of Liverpool and that NEC dressing room, the constituent parts of George had been totally re-arranged and he had become subsumed into another species... a species to whom the likes of me was at best, a pesky embarrassment, and at worst, a threat to their continued well-being.

After we had played our set that night, George came on stage and did some rock 'n' roll numbers along with every one else – Robert Plant of Led Zeppelin, the Applejacks, Denny Laine, Jasper Carrot, Roy Wood, Steve Gibbons, Noddy Holder, Dave Edmunds – the stage was choc a bloc with stars.

Yes the second meeting at George's house was no less nerve racking for me than the first. I felt like I was tripping over my tongue the whole time, but ex-Beatle George was the perfect host.

We sat around drinking our canned beers while he explained the history of the castle and the estate, a veritable Garden of Eden in downtown Oxfordshire. George treated Mik and myself to a boat ride around the grounds and then it was time to eat.

We found ourselves in a humble kitchen where we met Olivia, George's wife, and Rachel, the maid. The kitchen was a totally functional room with utensils and pans hanging on the wall and cookers, stoves and sinks along one side. In the middle, a big old country table was laid out ready for the meal.

"It used to be the servants quarters but we use it nearly all the time now" George told us.

We sat around the long table eating and chatting, pretenders to squiredom in stately residence barely a longboat ride from the earthy seat of the English realm itself. Called to dine with a King crowned by the renown of battles won, a Knight of the noble house of Beatle, whose exploits raised the hearts of men far and wide, whose glory spread to the distant reaches of the entire globe.

I pinch myself – yes I am here, and this is the man who once sat at the top of the known universe but today, just today, he is sat with us chewing the fat in this scullery parlour.

George seemed to me, a natural recluse, a man content to look back on what he'd done and in no hurry to do anything remotely like it again. Interested more in nature and the seasons, and a continuing search for meaning and purpose... Not a man chastened or wearied by his travels, simply a man who had travelled, but was thankful for having arrived. George exuded that air of gentleness, which I hazard to guess, he had always had. He reminded me very much of my friend Richard Tandy in this, and in his playful hermit-like contentment, unruffled and determined to stay that way.

After dinner, we all signed the visitors' book waiting for us in the hall, and then proceeded up the ornate staircase to 'the music studio'. A cassette tape lying on a desk seemed to jog George's memory: "Ah Jeff, I've had this tape sent to me... it's an old Buddy Holly song... I'd like to play it".... We all listened to 'Peggy Sue got married' and George asked Jeff if he would help produce a version of it with him singing:

"I thought maybe you could sprinkle some of your magic dust on it!"

"Oh that's a great song" I proffered, like a show-biz impresario giving priceless advice to his protégé.

(It must have sounded crass, but I meant it. I've always had a special love for that song – it was one of the first I ever learned to play! A lifetime later, when Mandy and I were looking for a musical way to tell our story, we plumbed for 'Peggy Sue got Married'. We use it with a great long intro which I talk over about how I learned to play guitar).

We followed George through a door into what he proudly called "the guitar room." It certainly was. Every piece of wall area was taken up with guitars of all shapes, size and pedigree. Tons of them, all hanging there like priceless paintings. It was like being in The Louvre after closing time. One of them caught my eye – a Rickenbacker 12 string. A film shot from years before flashed through my mind, George playing *that* guitar...

"Excuse me – is that the one you played Hard Days Night on?" I asked, staring gloatingly in homage.

"Yep, this is the one" said George, picking it off the wall. Suddenly, I remembered a bit of that song that I, and no one else I knew, could ever figure out...

"Er... can you show me how you played the lick at the end of that record?" He seemed delighted to be asked.

"Oh that, that's simple" he said.

He played it and I stared at his fingers. I could hear the tune, it was just like the record, I could see him doing it, but I still couldn't figure it out!

George spotted my bewilderment and, motioning me closer, played it one note at a time, explaining each one. Suddenly the penny dropped!

A twelve-string guitar has six pairs of strings, each pair sitting close together. Four of the six pairs have strings tuned in octaves to each other. Normally you just strum across them both to get the '12-string' sound, but if you pluck just one of the pairs downward, you get a different octave than if you pluck it upwards!

That was the secret of how George played the lick on the end of 'Hard Days Night'.

I just looked at him and smiled. It was so stunningly simple, what can you say?

When Columbus returned from discovering America, a detractor in the royal household back in Spain said something like this to him:

"That was no big deal – all you had to do was sail west until you came to it!"

Columbus replied: "Yes, you are right, it is easy when someone else has shown you the way!"

That night in Henley ended with us all sitting around, beer cans and guitars at the ready.

"Play us one of yer classics Jeff, and I'll play yer one of mine" said George.

Classics never came better shod.

Hello Robert

Being part of ELO meant getting invited to parties, many at the sumptuous residences of the famous – as well as Jeff Lynne's castle-cum-home in Meriden there were parties at Bev Bevan's house, at comedian Jasper Carrot's, and then one night at Robert Plant's countryside retreat south of Birmingham. Robert had made the big time as the singer of the supergroup 'Led Zeppelin'.

I didn't think he would remember the guy who had been thumbing a lift on the Halesowen by-pass one night in the sixties, and him stopping to give me a lift in his battered old van with 'Band of Joy' daubed on the side in a big coloured script that looked like it had been painted by a three year old. But I remembered him and that van. The inside of it had all the functionality of a junk yard – a kaleidoscope of bits of equipment – motoring and musical – amongst which, within which and upon which young Robert and the members of his group, perched like stowaways in the bowels of a tramp steamer. It was cramped, dark, noisy and smelly. We made our acquaintance as we trundled along, exchanging small talk about the local group scene before wending our separate ways into the night.

But now he was a megastar and as I walked across the grounds of his Warwickshire home, I could see the unmistakable locks of his long blond hair atop his large frame standing in a glazed porch way, greeting the guests as they filed up to him like it was a royal investiture, which in a way, it was.

I studied the protocol: The invitees were presenting themselves in ones and twos while those immediately behind, at the head of the line, stood back a polite distance as private words were exchanged between host and guest. A stream of commoners full of nervousness and expectation, waiting behind the line on the floor to have their passports stamped…

We joined them in the ante-chamber of the porch and I fell in behind Richard, knowing that he would be familiar with the drill for these occasions. "Follow Richard and you can't go wrong" the inner voice said…

Richard walked forward and said something, offering his outstretched hand to be shaken. I was sure I heard him say

"Hello Richard" but decided I must have misheard him because I didn't think Richard would have gotten his name wrong. Anyway, it was obvious that Robert Plant knew Richard Tandy because I distinctly heard him say "Good to see you Richard" as he shook his hand with a warm smile. And why not? Richard was a star too. Not with the same notoriety of image maybe, but a chap who like Robert had been called up from the gutter to the lofty heights of the new English class that rock 'n' roll had created.

I stepped across the imaginary line and moved up. 'Hi Robert' I said – and to my horror he replied:

"Hello Robert, thank you for coming!" and immediately I realised in a moment of smouldering dismay just what the protocol of greeting royalty is: You introduce yourself with YOUR name, not theirs!

But anyway it proved one thing. He had no recollection of the fellow musician whom he had given a lift to all those years ago, and even if he did, he now thinks his name is Robert.

Tandy Morgan

It was always a problem – what to call ourselves. Richard and I racked our brains to think of suitable moniker which we could live with, and appellations bounced between us like a shuttlecock at a Chinese table tennis tournament. But eventually we tired of all the exotic, convoluted constructions we came up with and decided to render ourselves simply as 'R & D'. Apart from standing for Richard and Dave, this was also shorthand for Research and Development, which nicely described the state of play in our little group. And so under the banner of 'R & D' we had a record out called 'Berlin' in 1984.

Two years later when both the 'Action' charity record and the previously recorded 'Earth Rise' album was released by the small Wolverhampton-based heavy metal label that Tony Clarkin had introduced us to, we became 'Tandy Morgan'. Later still in 1992, when the ELO fan club suggested putting out the tracks that Martin and I had put together at Grimm Doo in the late 80s, we added his name to become 'Tandy Morgan Smith'. By this time the Compact Disc had superseded vinyl records, and the amount of recording time that could be squashed into the new format increased from forty to over seventy minutes. We decided to take advantage of the new technology and give the fans a value for money and used all the available space with 17 tracks of music. Sheila came up with the title for it – "Why don't you call it the B.C Collection?" she said as we all turned with "why?" written on our faces – "you know, BC as in

'Before Christ'!"' That was it. 'The B.C Collection', released in 1992, was composed of songs that had been written before I became a Christian in 1988.

Wedding May 4, 1982.

At the reception, some impromptu music at the Strathallan Hotel

Left:
Music at the Strathallan - myself, Jeff and Jim Cleary.

Below:
Nothing Says Hello like a smile 1982 Jim Cleary and Pam.

Publicity foto for release of 'Berlin' on the Sonet label, 1984. Richard and Dave under the name 'R & D.' Foto Copyright Sonet Records

At the entrance of Ridge Farm Studios, Sussex, with Richard and Brian Leahy

Richard and Steve Lipson in the studio.
"....and we were wondering if you would like to work with us again?"

Left: rehearsing with Richard at Grimm Doo.

Mom

Tandy-Morgan-Smith. Martin. Me, Richard and Sheila at Grimm Doo

Action 18 March 1986

At Birmingham's Town Hall on Saint Patrick's day, members of local bands gather as bow-tied guests of the CBSO (City of Birmingham Symphony Orchestra), for a special photograph to be taken by Lord Lichfield. The cast includes: UB40, John Lodge of the Moody Blues, Jeff Lynne of ELO, the Tandy-Morgan Band, Ruby Turner, 'Hooked on Classics' man Lou Clark, Bob Catley of Magnum, Steve Gibbons. Each had made a contribution to the 'Action' LP, which was released alongside the Tandy-Morgan single of 'Action' (produced by Jeff Lynne), all in aid of the Children's Hospice Appeal.

Photo Copyright Metro News

Rehearsing at the Boggery, Solihull, one cold day early in 1986. Martin and Richard - with his scarf on.

The mind boggles. What is Richard doing? Is he pleading with the crowd at this German concert? Are they worshipping him or are they angry?

The ultimate 'Hello Mom' pic: My mush appears on the giant screen at the side of the Wembley stage set. Someone was kind enough to snap this shot for me,

Wembley 4 July 1986. Backstage at Wembley the day before the concert. (Jeff can just be seen peering mischievously at the camera over Bev's shoulder). In the centre is sound engineer Colin Owen, at right, Phil Hatton, Jeff's personal roaddie.

13 July 1986. The end of an era. Phil Hatton took this shot of us all in the bowels of the concert hall at Stuttgart just before the last ELO gig.

SEVEN – FLYING

Flying aeroplanes and getting up to play on a stage for me, have one thing in common:

Every time is like the first time! Oh you might have done it a thousand times before, but if ever you get to the point where you feel blasé about it, that's the time it will come and show you that you're just a beginner.

They both seem to be endeavours where an inordinate amount of time is spent hanging around in a torpor of boredom waiting for something to happen. Then, when something finally does happen, you find yourself catapulted into the opposite extreme, an all too brief slice of time spent working at 110% in a whirlwind of intense nervous activity.

But then afterwards… Ah! When the wheels touch down; when you step off a platform back onto mundane reality, back into the benevolent service of gravity, that's when you know why you do it.

The fact is both flying and getting up in front of people is one part ordeal and two parts blessing and privilege. Both never cease to be a challenge to me.

Aerobatics

Kevin was a fellow musician who used to frequent the 'Rum Runner' night-club where I played with Magnum. No sooner had I got my Private Pilot's Licence in 1974 than I began canvassing pals who set foot in the club with the question: "would you like to go flying with me?"

Kevin jumped at the idea and was immediately hooked by it. We spent a lot of time flying around together and often, when we were safely aloft, I would show him how to do various things. Really it was the result of flying with Kevin that first invoked in me the astral notion that one day, maybe I could teach people how to fly.

Before very long, Kevin's interest in flying had propelled him to take up a course of training himself. He was a star pupil, going solo after just four hours of instruction. It was an all-time record for the flying club at Birmingham. Apart from his natural aptitude, he always accredited this to the time he spent being unofficially coached by me.

But as soon as he completed his training and got his own licence, his love for flying took off in a big way. Kevin quickly zoomed past me in the number of flying hours and qualifications he amassed. Before long he had obtained an Instructor's rating, then an Instrument rating, then a Commercial Licence, then he sold his stationery business and purchased a flying club at Birmingham. One day he suggested to me that we go up together in the aerobatic Cessna he had just acquired for his flying club, so that he could show me the aerobatics he'd just learned.

We climbed into the little machine. The cockpit was distinguished from the non-aerobatic variety by an industrial array of heavy-duty seat straps replete with military-looking buckles. Being strapped in was an experience in confinement which brought to mind being a guest of the electric chair.

We got airborne and aimed ourselves into the 'FIR' – the Flight Information Region – safely away from Birmingham's busy airspace. Kevin immediately set about imparting to me some of the tricks he had learned. It turned into as much a lesson in English as one in aeronautics:

"I'll talk through a barrel roll" he said, and began diving the aircraft while giving a running commentary to explain what he was doing:

"Now I pull back and raise the nose fifteen degrees. Now check…" (I thought I wonder what 'check' means – it must mean check the nose is where it should be before the next bit.) "Now full aileron and some rudder."

The sky quickly rotated in unison with my stomach and we were thrown this side and that in the little cockpit before finally everything went back right-side up, blue sky up above, brown earth below.

"Right, now you have a go!"

Kevin talked me through as I took over the controls:

"Dive the aircraft. That's right, now pull back, raise the nose fifteen degrees, now check!" (There he goes again with that 'check' thing – I thought – ah well, the nose is where it should be...)

"Now full aileron and some rudder" he intoned over the gale of wind noise. The sky began to rotate in an entirely novel fashion as we both gazed out of the window, buffeting against each other.

"What are you doing?" he yelled as we found ourselves looking down at the blue sky – and up at the brown earth. We were hanging by our straps, upside down, as the aircraft slowly ran out of energy. It tottered there for a couple of seconds while the two of us pushed and pulled the controls like bumbling idiots in a Hollywood comedy, all the while shouting at each other. Finally, the little machine collapsed into a corkscrew dive, performing what must have been an un-catalogued manoeuvre, before eventually coming to a state of equilibrium right-side up.

"You didn't *check*!" said Kevin accusingly, while we both giggled nervously at the clumsy arc we had just described through the sky.

"Well, what exactly do you mean by *check*?" I shot back.

"It means you pull back and then *check*! – STOP pulling back!"

"Oh" I said, duly corrected, and we both laughed and jibed at each other with insults and blame for the incompetence of the whole spectacle.

Once the significance of the word *check* had been duly etched on the tablets, Kevin continued on with his display of aerobatic prowess. He seemed to enjoy making all the manoeuvres as fierce as possible, something which I have never cared for. The whole exercise left me with no longing to take up aerobatics myself.

Hector

As Richard Bach wrote: "You always teach best what you most need to learn."

I found I had a flair for teaching people to fly. Really it was only because my appetite for learning it myself was so ravenous. And so eventually I took the course of training to become a flight instructor.

Like a motorists who must sport 'L' plates on their car, a flying instructor in England must first work in reduced capacity as an 'Assistant Instructor'. This meant being under the supervision of a more qualified person, a device that meant you could not, for example, send a student for first solo.

In 1979 I spent the summer at Humberside Airport, learning how to be an assistant instructor.

"We can give you guidance as to how to instruct" the man had said, "but we can't show you how to teach. Your students will do that!"

("What a cop-out" I thought, "that's exactly what I'm paying you all this money for!")

But how true it is. I was later to discover for myself that students do indeed show you how to teach – and how not to teach – as indeed I, as a bungling pupil, had shown Kevin that day.

However I wanted to tell you about Hector...

Hector was a wizened old man of about 80 years of age, a legend in the British flying fraternity. When I first met him at East Midlands Airport in October 1979, he was stood gazing out of a window, a cigarette permanently wedded to the fingers of one hand, a cup of tea occupying the other.

I introduced myself – Yes, I was the bloke booked in to be tested for the issue of an Assistant Flying Instructors Rating, I proudly confirmed.

He looked back out of the window and up at the sky.

"Hmmm. It's a nice day for aerobatics David" he said with his thin shaky voice, "would you like to do some aerobatics?" His voice sounded for all the world like a Spike Milligan impression.

(Aerobatics – Ugh! The thought of hanging upside down by the straps again passed before me...)

"Er, no thanks" I said cowardly.

"Oh" said Hector, the friendly smile fading from his face.

The atmosphere changed as suddenly and surely as if my words had caused the sun to go behind a cloud.

"Right" he said coldly, "well, off you go, check the plane over please and I'll be out in five minutes."

Soon Hector and I were ensconced in the little Cessna and he was giving me a list of things he wanted me to do. What had before been the squeaky little membrane of an inoffensive old man had suddenly gathered all the fearsome gravity of a Richard Burton oration... Hector had turned into a monster.

He remained so for the duration of the test, even slapping my hand after we had landed and I reached to retract the flaps:

"Don't EVER let a student see you do that – one day it will be the undercarriage lever!" he roared scoldingly.

I thought: "That's it! My first instructor's test and I've failed!"

"Pull off here" snarled Hector pointing to a taxiway.

The aircraft came to rest and I began running through the after-landing drills, trembling inside.

"Yes, well that's all right David," he said, his voice singing sweetly – the change took me by surprise. It had gone back to the Spike Milligan impression again.

"What – you mean I've passed?" I asked incredulously.

"Yes, of course David. No problem. Park the aircraft over there please, and we'll go and have a chat, get a cup of tea and write up the forms."

The next time I arrived for the instructor's test with Hector it was like a déjà vu experience:

He was stood by the same window, clutching the same omnipresent cup of tea and cigarette. He gazed up at the sky and said exactly the same thing:

"Nice day for aerobatics David. Would you like to do some aerobatics today?"

"Yes please" I said, and the spell was broken. The sun carried on shining and Hector beamed back at me.

"Shall I go and check the plane over?" I asked.

"No, that's okay" he said, stubbing out his cigarette, "we'll do it together"

Hector was a different man.

I sat watching the world turn around like I was watching TV. There was hardly any 'g' loading – the thing that makes your stomach reposition itself to somewhere just under your chin – it was the exact opposite of the ungainly fairground ride that Kevin and I had before. Of course, Hector was a past master at the art of aerobatics and Kevin, by comparison, had been but a beginner.

I got to do several annual renewal tests with Hector and got used to the drill: If he asked to do aerobatics I always said "Yes".

One time while we were airborne on a test, he asked me if I had ever heard the 'Blue Danube' played on the Stall Warner. Now the Blue Danube is of course, a Strauss waltz, and the stall Warner –

well, that is a device fitted to the airplane that blares out in an ungraceful 'honk' when the aircraft approaches the stall.

"Er, no I don't believe I have ever heard that played on the stall Warner Hector" I said bemused, wondering what on earth was coming next.

"I have control" he said, and then began humming the first bit of the Blue Danube tune: "Da da di da da" – and then suddenly, he pulled back so quickly and violently on the controls that the stall Warner followed on in perfect timing with 'Honk-honk, Honk-honk'.

After the flying there was the oral test where he would seek to discover the extent of a student's knowledge base, always with the cleverest of questions, couched in his playful and wacky way:

"If you and I were in jail for a long time David, I dare say we would get to talk about flying quite a lot – you know to pass the time away. Maybe one day I might be discussing with you why it is that maximum control deflection can be made at a higher speed in a heavily laden aeroplane than in the same aeroplane when it is lightly loaded. It's strange isn't it? Would you be able to tell me why that is David?"

That is how Hector would eke out of you the bounds of your aviation wisdom. He sometimes asked for hard facts, but more often asked the sort of question that betrayed your intuition, or lack of it, for aeroplanes and the atmosphere they inhabited.

Yes, Hector Taylor was a wonderful old-timer of the Spitfire vintage. Like every instructor I have ever flown with, I always learned a lot from him.

First Solo

"Okay off you go. One circuit only please. Just do everything the same as you've been doing and er… don't forget …" there is the sudden check list of things which looms and falls like an avalanche, usually ending with: "and I'll be watching you" – although not spoken remotely like a threat and certainly not with any tone of concern; just the platitude of mom shoving her baby on stage with her angel costume pinned just so and her fairy wand stood ready to dance in time to the script of ten words that she has never yet quite spoken in the right order, but never mind, she has in fact spoken them. So darling off you go, once around the crib please, remember your lines and try not to crash into Gabriel and mommy will be right here and you're gonna do just great, and never let it be alluded to that mommy will be beside herself in mortified dread until you come back and then she will be rendered perfect in a state of bottomless joy if, or should I say when, you return victorious from the footlights with or without honour, just with your costume and smile intact.....

The slipstream from the prop tugs at the door bidding you to close it and you turn to do just that but then an afterthought commands that you dive back inside the little cockpit:

"Oh and I've left my map here on the seat. No, of course you don't need a map to do one circuit of the aerodrome but it is a legal requirement that you carry it."

You nervously think about cracking the sick joke about it being repatriated in an uncharred condition, or the one about its usefulness in finding the way back from the Irish Sea. But no.

"Do you really think I am ready?"

"Of course you are. You'll be fine."

Slam.

The door closes and you walk away in a stride of royal confidence while inside you are shrivelling around the knot that has invaded the place where your stomach is usually found. You wonder how it is you can dare to make such bold predictions – 'you will be fine' – and you think of all the little items you have forgotten to mention and all the other items you have rammed home with far too much verbal and far too little example and so in all probability, to zero avail.

But life is a wonderful thing. After all, life is a first solo.

The wheels leave the ground and you are committed to sit in your machine until you and it have fumbled around that wonderful racetrack of life's dramas and then, with help and maybe a pep talk from you, aimed back down that welcoming gulley of lovely black tarmac with white lines and a great big number painted on it, and on either side, grass and gravity and mom with a bar of chocolate.

A first solo is always preceded by the instructor's radio call asking the tower:

"Can you accept a first solo?" – which really is a coded way of enquiring if the fire department is on station and ready to ride their greasy pole or whatever else they need to slither down in order to get the foam squirting in short order. It is a legal requirement – that the fire team are ready to go – but of course you don't let on anything about that. You try to say it quick so that the student maybe misses it, but then any student alert enough to drive himself around the sky should be compos mentis enough to spot the strange radio terminology wafting past. I remember hearing my instructor say it as we taxied around Birmingham Airport that autumn day in 1973: "Can you accept first solo?" – and the bolt of adrenalin followed almost immediately by the spanner of denial – no I hadn't heard him right, I must have imagined it. For who wants to hear such a thing before its appointed time?

It was in 1993 that I completed the short course to upgrade from Assistant to Full Instructor, a nomenclature that carried the dubious privilege of being able to send students on their first solo.

A scan through my log book reveals that since then I have sent over fifty people first solo. I am pleased to report that all have returned with their costumes intact. But always it is an ordeal of special magnitude for the instructor as well as it is, of course, for the student.

Vulcanology

Outside the flying training club where I work at Stratford there is an aeroplane parked up, slowly trying to corrode away. It is no ordinary aeroplane, not even the same shape as most aeroplanes – it has no tail plane but instead one gigantic delta-shaped wing. It sits there, year in and year out, grandiose and resplendent in its blue and grey camouflage, like a sentinel guarding the club, the airport, the empire! (for sure it doesn't know the empire has faded and equally for sure no one has the heart to whisper such a blasphemy within its earshot).

It is a 'Vulcan' bomber and it is big. Its massive wing swallows up four engines of a type that became the basis for powering Concorde, and the whole delta shape of the Vulcan was a precursor to the supersonic design. The difference is the vintage – whereas

Concorde first appeared in 1969, the Vulcan is almost twenty years it's senior, first flying in 1952.

But there are dark things about this behemoth – the darkest being that it was designed to atom-bomb Russia. And its name – 'Vulcan' – is also suspicious, belonging to no English town, city or settlement that I know of. Not only is it *not* named after a town, it is also *not* named after Lieutenant Spock, as much as this knowledge will devastate the Trekkies amongst us.

On the ground it is a giant camouflaged gazebo which I often walk under between training details, gazing up at its cavernous bomb bay, lost in a daydream where I see it loaded up with nuclear nasties, it's engines revving away, while inside five freshly shaved young men talk numbers to each other in their professional clipped calm as they go off on their mission to end the world.

I climb inside it. In the cramped compartment, over to one side, is a metal box with 'HANDLE LIKE EGGS' stencilled on it. I ponder what manner of foul genie lay stowed in that container, waiting for the coded call to set it free. Up in the cockpit, I squat in one of the two ejector seats (the other three guys down below had to jump out of the bottom). A Red painted handle glares at me, daring me to pull it – a note suggests that the firing pins have been removed, but have they?? Around the windows, a thick nylon curtain lies coiled, ready to pull down when the bomb is dropped, so that you will be preserved from the blinding flash and able to see where you are going. Able to use your eyes to fly back home and see for yourself the black lifeless ruin it has surely become.

The Vulcan was the product of the Avro company but I have it on the authority of the Encyclopedia Maximus Galactica that ever since the invention of the catapult, all Avro company bombers have been named after an English city or town (most will remember the 'Lancaster', even if they've never heard of the 'Manchester' or the 'Lincoln'). The strange fact is, my extensive library of maps does not show a place called Vulcan anywhere in Great Britain.

But there must be one somewhere, because there is definitely an Avro Vulcan bomber parked outside our flying club. There must be a place called Vulcan, probably even a county called Vulcanshire. There must be citizens called Vulcans – or Vulcs for short, and the thing is, the more I ponder this machine, the more I think I am one of them!

For I belong in that place where memories live, where the past refuses to be pronounced dead, where the dead refuse to be buried, a place colonized by those among us who are stricken with the malady called 'nostalgia'. And it's not just me....

Looking out from the clubhouse, I constantly notice a curious thing: The Vulcan's final trip to the scrap heap is forever being put back by a dads-army posse of unsung heroes. These 'Vulcs' (they must be Vulcs), are Royal Air Force veterans who spend their own free time lovingly attending to the many demands of this venerable machine. After striking up conversations with the Vulcs I have become privy to many interesting snippets of information. 'Our' Vulcan is one of the last ones made – a 'B2' (that means bomber mark 2). I can reveal that a mark two is distinguished from a mark one by an extended tail which houses electronic jamming equipment, and small protrusions under each wing which, like the glint of a concealed dagger, are evidence of betrayal in high places, for these hide the stubs of pylons where the Skybolt stand-off missile was to have been attached. The Americans thoughtlessly went and cancelled Skybolt after Her Majesty's government had gone and built these planes to carry it!

But thankfully, the Vulcan was never called upon to fulfil its primary duty, and never dropped anything in anger except a few ineffectual bombs upon Port Stanley airport in the Falklands, in 1982 while I was busy getting married for the first time.

Yes, unrequited history is built into this aluminium artefact along with all the substance of drama, glory and heritage, and that is why these men scurry so tirelessly about it. For one day the glory must finally be gone, but please, let it not be today.

I understand that! But then, I am a Vulc

Parallel Universes

The phone rang:
"Mr. Morgan?"
"Yes"

"My name is Kennard and I'm attached to the Patent Office. I am calling with reference to the application you made on 25th November 1980, regarding 'wing tips'. Can you confirm it was you who made this application?"

"Er.. yes." (I am thinking: "Oh no, he's going to say stop wasting our time with your silly ideas".)

"Are you aware Mr. Morgan that under section 22, paragraph 1, of the patents act, the comptroller can prohibit publication of any application deemed to be of potential interest to the Ministry of Defence?"

"Er, yes I am" I had vaguely read something to that effect in the pamphlet.

"Well I am directing that be so in this case. As of now, you will not publish or communicate any information relating to this application to any person who has not been authorised by this office to receive it. Is that clear?"

"Y-yes."

He went on to ask me if I had already discussed it with any person or company and I told him I hadn't.

"Very well then, you will receive an official notification of this conversation by return of post. Is all that understood?"

"Yes."

"Thank you, good day!"

Mr Kennard's letter arrived the next day. I still keep it as a memento.

The wing tips idea ('Vortex Management Wing Tips' – a lofty name for a very simple idea) was an extra-musical project I was pursuing at the time. I had made some rough sketches and sent them off to the patent office as a provisional application. It was a shock to get the secret order slapped on it and of course it didn't last long: Some two months later the letter came saying that the defence of the realm could survive without my idea after all, and I could now tell the world about it.

The rigmarole of trying to obtain a patent was something I had already become familiar with a few years previous. The first 'idea' that I ever went the full course with was something that came to be called a 'Timescale'. – A printed piece of elastic fabric held in a plastic container, it looked a bit like a slide rule. The fabric had a scale of minutes printed on it and could be adjusted between a range of speeds, the whole arrangement being designed to correspond to the scale of aeronautical charts.

I had just got my Private Pilots Licence in 1974 and was planning cross-country trips, measuring the distance along sectors and then doing a sum on a circular slide rule to figure out how long it would take. Suddenly the brainwave came to me: What if I could make an expandable scale able to cope with the different speeds over the ground (according to whether the wind is for you, or against), then I could just read off the time by measuring it straight off the map!

"But does a strip of elastic fabric expand equally along its length?" I thought. I tried it out quickly, it worked. Eureka! I shot around to a friend's house with a hastily convened mock-up and showed him. He encouraged me with the look of someone who is not really sure if I needed hospitalisation or not…

That little invention became like Frankenstein's monster, a creature that took over my life. As well as running the gauntlet of a patent application, I ended up forming a limited company to manufacture the Timescale. By 1978 running the company was taking nearly all of my time.

I sold a lot of those 'Timescales' all over the world, making many interesting contacts doing it.

Hal Shevers in America was one. He owned the foremost shop for pilot accessories in America – in Cincinatti, Ohio. He was one of my biggest customers and when I went to the States with ELO, I called him up and told him I was about to start a USA-wide tour with a pop group.

"Oh really Dave, I didn't realise you were a musician" he said.

(Well I hadn't told him. Making gadgets for pilots and playing music in a pop group seemed like they belonged in parallel universes).

"Say, what's the name of the group you're playing with Dave?"

"They're called ELO."

"Sorry Dave, what was that?"

"E-L-O, it stands for the Electric Light Orchestra."

"Okay" he said in an uninterested monotone, "well if you make it to the Ohio area, give me a call. Maybe we can meet up."

It was early November when I looked at the schedule and realised we would be in Cincinatti on the sixth. I called Hal's office.

The secretary put me through with lightning speed and Hal's voice was suddenly singing down the line:

"DAVE!"

"Hello Hal..." I said, but he quickly interrupted:

"Dave... it seems I was the only person in the whole WORLD who didn't know who the Electric Light Orchestra was! When I asked the guys who work here if they'd ever heard of the name they went ballistic. Listen, is there any chance you can get any concert tickets for my staff, otherwise my name is mud around here?"

I told him I would see what was available and get back to him and then he asked:

"What airport are you flying into?" I checked the itinerary and told him.

"I'll be there to meet you!" he said.

And he was. He flew to meet us in his Piper Aztec and was waiting on the tarmac as our Viscount pulled up.

My future wife Pam was travelling with us for that part of the tour, and while the rest of ELO left in limos for the hotel, Pam and I departed in Hal's private plane. He chaperoned us via another small airport to his house and then on to the show at the Riverfront Coliseum. After the show there was a restaurant dinner with the staff from Hal's company (I think there were 26 in all who I had managed to obtain tickets for). The next morning he gave us a tour of his business (Sporty's Pilot Shop) before we rejoined the ELO airplane to fly to the next (and last) date in Bloomington, Indiana.

Making the Timescale work was for me, a joy. It took me up a learning curve that tested me, and stretched me so much I thought I would snap like the elastic that composed it. But in the end, the many technical difficulties and financial impediments were overcome and it became a reality.

But I have to admit, as it metamorphosed into a business, it slowly turned into drudgery. I became the pick-up truck, the invoice clerk, the packaging agent – everything I was never cut out to be. I suppose it would have been different had it actually made any real money, but although the developed Timescale worked great (it even got a write-up in Flight International), as a business it was a flop.

For a while I was imprisoned by the business machine I had created, a machine that was essentially a cripple. Some of the time while I was nominally a 'Managing Director of a limited company' I was also on the dole!

But the thing that was to unshackle me from this monster was totally unrelated and unexpected:

A telegram arrived one day in March 1979 (yes, those were the days when important news, good or bad, arrived by telegram). It simply said:

IF YOU WROTE HIROSHIMA PLEASE TELEPHONE
01-XXX-XXXX (a London phone number).

I phoned the number and was told that my song 'Hiroshima' had been in the German Top 50 for almost a year!

I had almost forgotten about it. The telegram caused me to remember that I had once been a songwriter! The sweat I had put into songs had come from the pores of my soul, whereas the Timescale had drawn me closer to middle earth where the normality gene thrives, songs could always claim the higher ground because they were dredged from a deeper well.

It was the recording of 'Hiroshima' that Lou Reizner had done with the group Wishful Thinking, the one that had made me grimace with dismay when I first heard it in 1970. The Germans loved it and had bought it by the bucket load! Apparently, it first got noticed because of listeners in East Berlin calling to request it on a West Berlin radio station! Such is the rhyme and reason of rock 'n' roll history – unfathomable! That a song about the ultimate weapon should find its only fertile ground straddling the ultimate divide of the time – The Berlin Wall.

The telegram had come from the German publisher who was hanging on to my royalties instead of sending them to Lou's attorney in New York. He suspected I might not get paid if he sent them on. Before long, with his help, a legal way was set up for me to receive royalties direct from him.

The money paid for a decent car, an eight-track Teac tape recorder, and a trip to America at the end of 1979. (I stayed at Corky's for Christmas and New Year and then flew over to Los Angeles to meet up with Richard Tandy and Jeff Lynne, who were busy recording 'Xanadu'.) I still ran the Timescale business but it slowly wound down like a rusty flywheel – and I had no more energy to spin it up again. In 1982 I sold the whole thing to an Australian.

Some years later, in 1988, I was pursuing another idea, which I really expected Mr. Kennard to call about, but he never did. My 'Force-Generating Apparatus' (as the patent application was somewhat anti-septically labelled) is a revolutionary contraption, which although I have spent a lot of time and money on, has simply not worked – yet!

It is a sort of 'engine' – I call it a 'gyroscopic displacement unit'. Years ago I left the prototype stored at Richards' house. He called up one day asking did I want to collect it. – 'It sure is heavy for an anti-gravity machine' he said!

But I still harbour hopes of making this idea work one day.

Airtax

The Timescale had not long evaporated from my horizon when along came the 'PC' – the Personal Computer – and by the mid 80's I had acquired an interest in writing computer programs. At the time, my flying mate Kevin wanted a routine to work out flight quotations for his air taxi business and I developed one for him. My first wife Pam came up with the name for it: 'Airtax'. By the late 80's it had grown into a whole suite of programs for the aviation market, and for a couple of years in the early 90's, these sold like hot cakes. One day an order came in to send a copy of 'Airtax' to an outfit in Saudi-Arabia called Bin-Laden Aviation who, if my memory serves right, operated HS-125 business jets. It wasn't until some ten years later that the name took on its infamous cadence – Bin-Laden, a real life Doctor No – and I recalled with a cringe the ephemeral connection I had back then with the master of terror.

Kevin had been the prime mover in establishing the technical requirements for the 'Airtax' programs – his company was the flagship user of it and he actually changed the call sign of his company aircraft to 'Airtax'. Years later he sold the company and all its accoutrements, including the call-sign, to another operator based at Birmingham and it just so happens that later I worked as a Commercial pilot for that company, with the call sign 'Airtax', the name that Pam thought up all those years ago.

The genesis of an 'idea' is a process not dis-similar to writing a song – it's a notion that comes in the night, in the morning, in the bath, in the lift, on the bus, anywhere ...

Like a song, a new idea is always the most fragile of things. A cob web, you see it for a second, then you move your head, or the wind blows, and it's gone. It can take a lot of stubborn sweat before you can hang your cob web against a backdrop where anyone else can see it.

Ideas are no more than dreams, voyages into a reality that may or may not exist when you wake up, or if you are awake already, then when you snap out of it! The pursuit of a dream always takes you to places you could never imagine. Some of the journeys are fruitful and some are a complete waste of time, but the fun is in the travelling not the arriving. I consider it a bountiful gift to have been able to birth some of the ideas – some of the dreams that I have been allowed to dream.

Compost Heap

For a while I thought that I had dreamed up the title for this book, but in fact it's a line in Carl Sagan's novel: 'Contact'. I honestly don't remember reading it, but there it is, in a line of dialogue: '... the patterns in the chaos'. Maybe it's because of the compost heap syndrome...

I have always been of the opinion that many people probably make up songs. They hum a little ditty to themselves. Maybe they catch a phrase, or else some inspiration drops into their spirit – something of special or personal weight – and they play with it like a rosary bead as they walk along the road, never thinking it's worth anything. I know, that's exactly what I thought about it for years: "This song can't possibly be any good – I made it up!"

But you can't get serious about doing anything for too long before you become 'professional' – and for a writer that means becoming proficient at being a certain kind of sleuth – the kind that is a raving kleptomaniac preying on ideas. When you are a songwriter everything you hear becomes a potential lyric or maybe a title. The most mundane conversation if it hits you right, can throw up a line that gets wedded to a song. Nothing is safe. In my experience the trick of being a writer is to become a kind of compost heap into which everything goes, to get sifted through later and maybe used as fertiliser.

It was Richard Tandy – always on the lookout for a fitting ode – who told me about Buckminster Fuller's quote: "If you're not confused by what's going on in the world, you're not thinking straight." I promptly refashioned it and put it into the song 'City Girl' (released on the album 'The B.C.Collection'): 'And if you aint confused, there's something wrong with you'.

It's the compost heap syndrome, I can't help it! – Sorry Buckminster (is that really your name?).

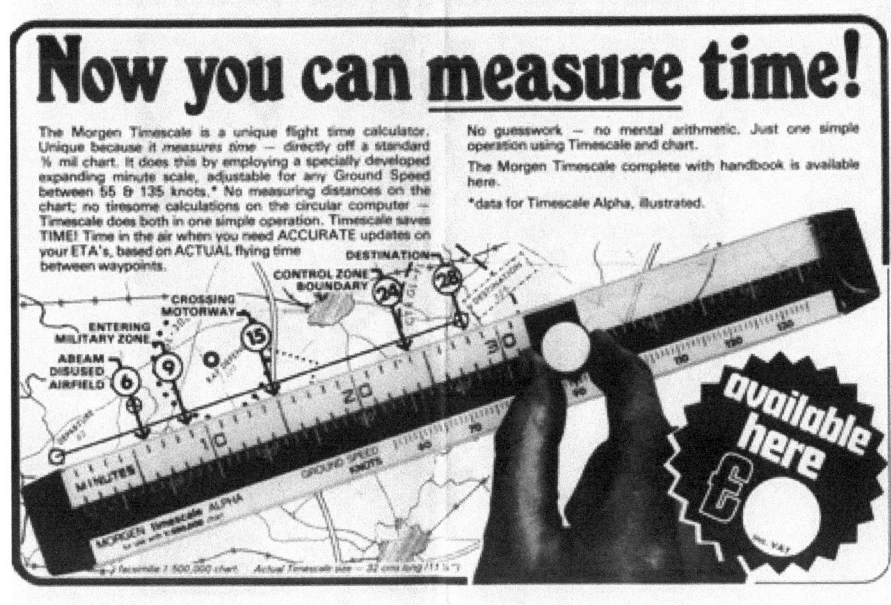

The 'Timescale' pilot navigation aid. The advertisement above was printed in Flight International in 1977 and created a lot of interest.

Left: Karen and I sailing between Greek islands.

Cover of the Extended Play version of 'Berlin' released in 1984.

Newspaper photo marking the release of 'Action' 1986. Martin Smith, Jim Simpson (drummer), myself and Richard Tandy.

EIGHT – ALCHEMY

May the Fourth be with you

While the British were fighting to recover the Falkland Islands from Argentina in 1982, I was busy getting married for the first time.

I had met Pam near to the beginning of ELO's 'TIME' tour – she actually picked me up in the most romantic manner by chasing me around gaming machines in a Las Vegas hotel lobby:

It was 18 September 1981, a few days after the start of the American tour and ELO had just jetted in from Fort Worth, high on our fame and good fortune, me higher than most. The lobby of the Aladdin in Las Vegas was laid out like a supermarket, with aisles crammed full of one-arm bandits. I'd never seen anything like it – it was a teeming bazaar of beings doing battle with row upon row of burping, winking robots. People sat on stools transfixed like zombies, pulling handles while staring intently at the strange hieroglyphics which forever betokened the promise of the next pull being the last you'll ever need.

As Richard and I negotiated our passage through the crowded aisles toward the lifts, I noticed a girl playing a machine seemed to be the same girl I'd seen in the previous aisle. Sure enough as we came to the last aisle, she re-appeared around the far end and quickly insinuated an interest in another machine along our line of travel.

That was how I met Pam: "Didn't I just see you back there?" I said as I passed her again.

"Who me?" she said with a beaming innocence.

She was a beautiful black-haired lady of American Indian descent. I came to know her as a person without negatives, a free spirit and pillar of strength. She never got depressed, in fact the word 'depression' was not in Pam's vocabulary. My Mom loved her, and why not? She was a joy to be around. She was forever "Yes" while I was forever "definitely maybe".

"Will you come to New York?"
"Yes".
"Will you come to England?"
"Yes".

"Will you marry me?"
"Yes".

And so it was that seven months after we met, we were married in Birmingham on May the fourth, 1982.

"May the fourth be with you" joked Richard in homage to the famous 'Star Wars' line.

There was a short clip on the local TV evening news about it, but the main news that day brought the word 'Exocet' into our vocabulary – it was the day the British Cruiser 'Sheffield' was sunk in the South Atlantic.

At the reception, Jeff Lynne, Jim Cleary, Richard and myself all got up, togged out in posh suits at the Strathallan Hotel, to play music to the gathered guests.

My marriage to Pam lasted two years and the reason it failed was my womanising and depressions. I was a serial womaniser and that, coupled with my bouts of communication blackouts, defeated our marriage. Nobody else was to blame but me. I had somehow thought that being in the ambience of her eternal optimism would heal me of my demons. But it didn't, it just painted over the cracks for awhile.

I met my second wife Karen on a blind date in 1984: A friend had popped into my house one night and we were both at a loose end. He suggested we could maybe meet up with a couple of girls he had recently met at the 'Elbow Room' night club. Out came his 'black book' of phone numbers and before long, two girls were knocking at the door. One was Karen. I never dreamed I would fall in love with her, but before long, that's what happened.

Then one day, equally unscheduled, she announced to me that she was leaving to marry her boss! I was gutted. I pursued her with letters and messages and songs and finally she came back.

By the time we got back together I was healed of being a serial womaniser. Karen was the first lady I never cheated on.

New Light

After ELO played its last gig in 1986, I had busied myself with various musical projects and in 1987, I got involved in writing and recording the soundtrack for a Hollywood film called 'Distortions'. It sounds great, but it turned into an epic bad experience for me. In a word, it was horrible – the film was horrible, the people were horrible, I was horrible, – and to cap it all, I didn't get paid for it! I came away with a cartload of bitterness toward the man who had hired me.

It was June 1988, I still hadn't been paid for the film and my blood boiled whenever I thought about it. By this time mom was disabled, living in a nursing home and wheelchair bound. She asked me to take her to a church that was just around the corner from where she lived. So, off we went: I remember everyone looked so infuriatingly blissful as I wheeled her into the Cadbury Hall in Selly Oak, Birmingham, that evening. I thought: "Boy, what are these guys on?"

After some energetic singing, the pastor got up and announced:

"Tonight my sermon is on disappointment!" I gasped. Straight away he got my attention – I was the authority on the subject that night, it was oozing out of me. I was so bitterly disappointed with everything, and most of all, with myself. I had always thought that I could work it out – that no matter what, somewhere I had the resources to sort out my own life. That night I was prepared to accept the fact that I couldn't. I had proved it again and again, I was hopeless at it!

The Pastor – Dave Woodfield – launched into his sermon. I remember it was really good, and I was glued to his words (I was, after all, an expert on the subject!) but as I sat there listening the weirdest thing began happening – Somebody else starting speaking to me! Behind the preacher's words there was another dialogue going on – like a sub text. And it wasn't coming out of my thoughts at all, but from somewhere quite different. It was something outside of me speaking forcefully right into the very centre. I say 'speaking' but it wasn't in 'words', yet I could put words to it. I knew what the message was – I heard it loud and clear:

"You've been angry at me for years… You blamed me for your dad dying and you've been running away from me ever since!"

In an instant I came face to face with the Creator God, and I was scared. A powerful force was prising me open and reaching into a place deep inside… a place full of secrets, things that nobody but me and God could possibly know about! In that moment I felt my whole inner being rise up like some incandescent ethereal ghost. I squirmed as a huge spotlight was turned on me and I was suspended there, dangling before everyone stark naked, with every eye in the building looking at me! My shame filled the place and for an instant, I was helpless with trepidation.

How did He know all this about me? – How did He know where to find me? – How..?'

I don't know how long it was but I remember the thought coming. I remember the fear turning to awe, to wonder and then to peace. It came like a homing beacon, a wonderful thought. It was simply this:

Why should He bother? Why should the Almighty bother to come to Selly Oak, Birmingham, to speak with David Morgan about this?

There was only one answer: I knew it then; I felt it… Love.

The Pastor's words faded back into my world – he was winding up his sermon. I remember him saying "…Friends will disappoint you, business associates will disappoint you, *I* will disappoint you, but Jesus will never disappoint you."

Then, at the end of his sermon, Pastor Dave said: "Put your hand up if you want Jesus to be your Lord tonight", and my arm rose as if all by itself. Inside I prayed silently: "Lord Jesus, come into my life and help sort me out please." There were no big flashes and I didn't feel so very different. A short while later someone came to me and took me into the quiet part of the foyer and helped me to say another prayer. He used terms such as *forgive my sins*, make me *born again* (I thought Cliff Richards had made that up but I was later to discover them to be the words of Jesus). Really I doubted that things could change just because I'd said a few words asking Jesus into my life. But they did...

Driving home from the church, a voice spoke clearly into my mind. This time it *was* in distinct words. It simply said: "You don't swear any more". (It wasn't like a threat, more like a statement of fact). And that was it. I didn't have to think about it, or try even, I just stopped swearing! Before that, I was unable to put a sentence together without it being liberally laced with profanities. Soon, all my friends noticed: "Dave, you're talking different!"

I had always had a suspicion that God was out there somewhere, waiting to zap me. But when it happened it was not the terrifying thing I had supposed. It was more like stepping through a curtain and finding myself in another world, a vast alternate reality that had always been there behind the veil; A vista that was both new and revolutionary and yet, at the same time, as old and dependable as the hills...

It was a turning point for me, a point of reference, like the day BC changed into AD. I embarked upon a journey that was not to be without obstacles and yet has been the most wonderful journey of all. God supernaturally intervened in my life in a forceful personal way. He came and confronted me with an issue that I had not mentioned to another living soul. In fact, I didn't even know before that night that it is possible to be 'mad' at God.

Over the following months, Pastor Dave and I slowly became friends. In fact over the years he was to become an indispensable ally and source of good counsel to me. He moved up the ecclesiastical ladder to be in charge of many churches, and me – well, I eventually became a pastor myself. But that didn't just 'happen' – there was a lot of kicking and screaming first....

Diamonds and Unexploded Bombs

It was late in 1988 that I began to feel that I ought to write a song about God (and mom, and everyone at church kept nagging me as well!). I tried several times but nothing came out, I didn't know where to start. In the end I thought "I just can't do this!"

I had a complete block about it, until one day – when I was out walking the dog, I came upon a soggy pamphlet lying on the pavement. It had 'GOD' in big red block letters on its cover. I bent down and picked it up, took it home and dried it out, opened it with curiosity, and read inside... As I read that little pamphlet, the words and music to 'Outside Jerusalem' came to me. It was as if it had just wafted up off the paper into my mind, and before many minutes I had written my first God song!

Sometime later I got to thinking about that piece of paper that dad had picked up off New Street all those years ago and its awful message. It's funny, the things you stumble on lying in the street.

Some can be like diamonds and some, like unexploded bombs. The first had been to me, a land mine that couldn't be defused, and the second, simply a gem, a gift when I needed it. Both came with the teaching that God is able to speak through anything, even something so bizarre as a scrap of soggy paper.

Another gift was that relations with mom slowly turned around – I don't know when or how exactly, but slowly we became the best of pals! All the past hurts were healed – changed even; Things that had seemed so bad years ago became things that I could actually be thankful for! The way she had looked after her brother Joe, and later married Alf – I came to see both in a new light. Mom's actions, which had seemed to so wound me then, claimed fresh significance and respect. Her actions and the way she would always speak words of faith and hope to people, made me glad to be called 'Vinnie's son'. Instead of hating her for her idiosyncrasies, I was proud of her. I didn't know it then but God so arranged it that before she died, mom was my best friend and I was her best friend. It is something I can never stop feeling grateful for.

Yes, there was some alchemy performed: structural engineering work; refurbishments and re-decorating. There had to be, to restore things to their rightful place. The whole experience was for me, something akin to stepping out of the Gulag into Disneyland. It was like hearing every Beatle song at once, before they were ever famous! It was every bit as exciting as being on tour with ELO. I entered an epoch of pure unadulterated joy.

Science calls it Epiphany (it always has a name for everything) and I emigrated from the land of cacophony into the land of epiphany in one sudden leap that evening in June 1988. I can only compare it with being in love.

The music began to take a whole new direction. Whereas before I couldn't fathom how to write a 'God song' at all, soon I found they were coming thick and fast. Before long I had a whole album of inspirational songs which I assembled onto a cassette tape called 'All God's Blessings' (a name unwittingly coined by a Romanian friend Emile, whose parting wave to us was always accompanied by those words).

Pastor Dave would encourage me to get up at church and sing the songs that I was writing. Some of these had backing tracks but by far the most successful Christian song I have ever written needed no such embellishment: 'This is my prayer' was a two part stanza that took me five minutes to write and required just a finger picked guitar to make it work. I remember playing it to Pastor Dave, not at all sure if it was any good. He didn't seem too sure either but nevertheless he said "play it this Sunday."

NINE – ROMANIA

It was early one July morning in 1990 when we crossed the border into Romania. We had set off from Birmingham four days before, myself and twelve other members of the church on Pastor Dave's expedition to take aid to Romanian orphanages and hospitals. It took ages for our convoy of one old coach and two vans to get through the frontier from Hungary but that was the norm. There were hundreds of others queuing in cars, lorries and buses, just the same.

The Communists had collapsed just seven months before in a popular uprising that had seen its leader and his wife shot in the courtyard of a military barracks.

Ceaucescu had been the absolute ruler of Romania, a modern day Pharaoh whose every whim was law. Life and death had flowed from him and his ruling clique as casually as a puff of wind, to be implemented by an army of lieutenants, each exercised by a level of fear from the next above. The only luxury was to be at some lesser station of oppression than somebody else. It was a system designed to grind the spirit of man to dust.

George Orwell never visited the place, yet he had described it to a tee. As we drove deeper into Romania, I soon began to feel like Winston Smith in Orwell's book 'Nineteen Eighty Four'. A piece of ash trapped in the furnace of blatant, all-encompassing madness.

O'Brien said to Winston: 'How many fingers am I holding up?' (he holds four).

'Four?'

'No, if the party says I am holding up five fingers, you must answer five, Winston'.

I was in the workers' paradise.

Oh boy, did I have to eat my words! I had often speculated that 'things aren't so bad behind the iron curtain' – thinking that we were victims to some measure of our own western propaganda. But I was wrong. Things…. big things, little things and all the in-between things, were immeasurably worse than I had imagined.

'Don't show me any purity' Winston said to his girl friend Julia, 'I just want to do it' (to have sex)…

Don't talk of beauty or virtue or anything like that, don't talk about that rubbish because this place could not exist if those things existed....

Romania was like a gigantic slave-labour camp, a multi-storey version of 'Schindler's List', an outpost of what President Reagan had accurately described as the 'Evil Empire'.

By July 1990 the monster that communism had created was still tottering along with the same old blood in its veins, stumbling in search of a transfusion that had to come from outside. And there we were, in an envious situation, foreigners on a coach, with tea and biscuits, and the ability to leave…

Pipeland

Soon after crossing the border we drove into the city of Oradea. It announced itself long before we ever reached it by a massive industrial plant stretching for miles along one side of the road. I looked out at a moving mural of shattered buildings – abandoned and vandalised I thought. Pipe-work exuded from everywhere. It was surreal, a gigantic Mad-Max science-fiction film set. The pipes spewed from it to join the road and become a sidewalk ornament that stretched out of sight into the distance. As our coach ambled past this sprawling facility I stared through the window and with shock, realised that it was not derelict, but a functioning factory! I saw people congregating outside its gates, waiting for a bus, and then noticed the people moving around inside its perimeter. It was just a factory in Romania, not a shattered, war damaged facility. This was … Normality!

When you read about slave labourers assembling state of the art V2 rockets for Hitler, something jars with the logic: You get the feeling of a short circuit in the brain – surely that cannot be! Surely rockets are put together in humidity controlled, spotless, air-filtered NASA sheds, not by starving forced labourers? Yet that is what happened in Germany.

Looking out at this, my first snapshot of the Romanian industrial infrastructure, I sensed the handiwork of that same perversity at work, and felt that same incredulity: 'this cannot be for real!' But it was.

Throughout our whole ten-day trip, I don't recall ever seeing a single thing that had a decent lick of paint on it. Everything was an unremitting shade of tatty grey. Everything was to some degree, like that ramshackle factory complex we passed at Oradea.

But as we began to meet the people it was impossible not to pick up on their warmth and willingness to help. They would drop everything and go out of their way to give us directions if we were lost, as we were, many times. The system had not ground them to powder. It had humbled them and brought them low. It had silently enraged them and made them a country of sneaks one upon the other. But it had not defeated them. They had defeated IT.

There were thirteen of us altogether, most of us riding in our big blue and white 1960's vintage charabanc – no doubt the conveyance of British Legion excursions to Rhyl in former times. 'Christian Life Centre' was emblazoned along its sides on giant stickers.

The trip to Romania had been organised by our Pastor, Dave Woodfield, the coach was donated by one of the congregation and the two vans by a local hire company. Dave had visited Eastern Europe, including Romania, many times before. Now, in the wake of the revolution, he had galvanised our church to respond to the frightful needs that had appeared as the veil of xenophobic secrecy collapsed to reveal the true impoverishment.

We sailed along like a caravan of gypsies, sleeping, eating and living out of our vehicles for much of the two-week journey. Our venerable charabanc looked like a mobile haberdashery shop: Every one of its luggage bays plus the inside rear (where the seats had been removed), was squashed tight with our cargo of goodies: All kinds of stuff – footwear and clothing, walking frames and invalid aids, wheelchairs, surgical equipments and supplies, even mobile lavatories! – a myriad of items donated by individuals and organisations in and around Birmingham. On our way we often came across other vans, lorries and cars from Britain and elsewhere, all similarly loaded. The Romanian tragedy had invigorated the conscience of the west, and we were one droplet in the torrent of supplies all flowing the same direction.

As we drove through villages, streams of children would run into the road and wave excitedly at us as if we were part of some victorious army column, whilst those older would stand back, some waving, some just looking on with amazement. The word had gone out: 'help is on the way!'

The uninviting visual hostility of the place which had screamed at me so aggressively when we first crossed the frontier, ebbed to a background murmur and soon, I felt completely secure in Romania. I found I could ask help from anyone, in my pigeon English-cum-Romanian, and be assured of a welter of attentions. The people treated us with great respect and their assistance was unconditionally and abundantly granted without any regard for their own inconvenience.

We plied our way through villages and cities, up and over the Carpathian mountain range, visiting churches and hospitals and disgorging our supplies to them. At every stop, armies of helping hands appeared from nowhere to help with the unloading.

Our northern-most point was the city of Suceava. We dropped off our supplies and then, with the majority of our cargo gone, we set off southward, driving through the night toward the Black Sea and Constanta, 300 miles away. We crossed the Danube just after dawn and reached the Black Sea coast by midday. By one o'clock we had found a piece of beach at Mamaia, a resort just north of Constanta. After the customary argy-bargy with the officials in charge we drove our vehicles onto the sand, corralled them into a semi-circle and pitched our tents alongside to spend a few days as tourists on the Black Sea.

Miti

It was the next day, Saturday 14th July, that something happened that was to influence my life greatly. Like all momentous events, it sneaked up from behind, or to be more accurate, from one side:

I was sat on a camping stool beside our coach, reading and smoking a cigarette quietly to myself. The rest were swimming in the Black Sea but I had had enough of the water for one day. I was all alone when up came this short, rather poorly dressed man:

"Excuse me" he said, "may I speak with you?"

"Er.. Yes, what about?"

"Oh no, not about anything... I just want to speak."

Each sentence was nervously thought about, composed and measured. He continued as I stared at him:

"I saw the union jack on your bus… and… I wondered… You are English, yes?"

"Yes."

"Ah good…. You see, I know English from the radio but I have never to speak it…"

He sat down and I asked him his name:

"Zaharia Chirica" he said.

"What?"

He repeated it slowly "Za-Ha-Ri-ah Keer-ee-kah," adding:

"That is my real name but I am also called 'Miti' – it is a sort of nick-name."

"Can I call you that please?" I asked.

He told me how he had learned English from listening to the BBC radio but wanted a chance to practise what he had learned. He just wanted to speak to an Englishman!

We must have spoken for about an hour when the rest of our party arrived in varying stages of wetness from their dip in the sea. Miti immediately got up to leave in deference to them and I quickly arranged to meet him later at the beach bar a short distance away.

"Who was that?" one of the girls in our party asked as she watched Miti walking away.

"Just a guy who wanted to have a chat." I replied.

"Is he a Christian?"

"I don't think so."

"Oh" she said darkly and turned away.

She wasn't interested. In fact nobody in our party took any interest in Miti, not then or later. I don't remember anyone else speaking to him even. I didn't understand it then. Much later I understood it perfectly: Miti had been sent to me, or rather, I had been sent to Romania to meet him!

We got to speak a lot those two days at Mamaia. As he struggled to invoke the correct words to communicate with me in English, I began to get the inkling that he was a deep well of understanding. We sat at the 'beach bar' (a complete misnomer, a ramshackle lean-to where beer – or as Miti described it 'slops' – was served by a disinterested, shabby bartender) and through the obstacle of culture and experience we found ourselves walking upon familiar tracks. We discovered we had much in common.

Miti came by Sunday morning and said he might be able to help us obtain gas for our camping stove. I drove with him to his sisters' flat in the nearby town of Navodari.

A dingy stairwell led us to a surprisingly well-appointed, comfortable small apartment. Miti introduced Helen, his sister, and her husband Rudi. They immediately disappeared in a noisy kerfuffle of chatter.

"Sit down please" Miti said to me, "make yourself comfortable." I sat down.

Helen re-appeared briefly, smiled and then disappeared in a gaggle of activity, taking Miti with her. Miti returned forthwith and said:

"Oh Dave please, you must not sit there!"

I got up apologetically, embarrassed that I had offended in some way, but Miti motioned to me to another seat:

"My sister says you must sit *here*"

I was directed to sit in the best seat in the house from people who didn't know me at all!

Soon, drinks and hastily prepared food arrived, proffered by Helen on a tray sporting neat napkins and fine cutlery. I just knew it was the best they had.

While I ate Rudi worked with Miti on our camping gas canister out on the small balcony, trying to transfer gas from his tank into ours. I finished eating and looked on. Without the correct union they were using their bare hands to try and form a seal around the valve, cupping them in a clenched prayer for a few seconds until the blast of pressurised gas froze their skin. I watched them as they took it in turns, one supporting the upturned full gas tank above the empty one, while the other made the connection for as long as he could. Eventually, they gave up with an avalanche of apologies. Rudi looked especially defeated:

"I am very sorry Dave, it is not possible."

I assured them not to worry, we would find the gas we needed somewhere along the road.

With Rudi and Helen and their three beautiful young girls waving good-bye, I set off with Miti back to our makeshift sandy habitat.

By midday, the Christian Life Centre entourage had decamped and after a short service on the beach, I said good-bye to Miti and we headed off for the capital, Bucharest, and the adventure of the long journey back to England.

Letter from Romania

Not long after arriving back home I received the first of many letters from Miti. His words were a mine of revealing information, always etched onto the flimsy, grey material that passed for Romanian writing paper. Miti had a flair for language that was explosive. He would write to me the most amazing exposés of the communist epoch along with remarkable insights into present day Romania. Although his grammar was often topsy-turvy, his use of words was magical. So much so, I decided to show a portion of one of his letters to a newspaper publisher in Birmingham.

I had known Mark Higgett from the days of 'Action' project (which his newspaper, the 'Metro News' had sponsored). Mark immediately picked up on Miti's unique style and said he would like to publish something; Could I get a photograph?

Hasty letters were transmitted to Romania to tell Miti of this new situation, and frankly, to give him an 'out' if he wasn't comfortable with it. The era of the Secret Police was only a hiccup behind, and I wasn't sure if his scathing words about the Romanian experience, along with his photograph, in a foreign newspaper was wise. (I remembered well how he had told at Mamaia that if ever he was to bump into a foreigner in Ceacescu's time, he had to report it immediately to the police, along with everything that was said!)

But Miti was not to be deflected by the fear that had once infected his country and supplied two photographs – one of himself, and another of him with his mom. The article was published in a massive spread across two inside pages of the Metro News on 11 October 1991:

'The bleeding heart of a broken land' it said in massive type, and beneath it as a sub-heading: 'Letters from newly liberated Romania'.

To lend a bit of local perspective, Mark included a small bit about me, and how I came to meet 'Mytty' (as he spelled his name). My photograph was captioned 'Dave Morgan: Chance meeting'. How true that was.

It was during this time that I used to fly as a check pilot for George Wilkins, a local businessman. George had shown interest in my Timescale invention way back when it was in its infancy: (in the mid seventies he had commissioned and bought a specially produced prototype off me for the princely sum of £50!). One day after we had landed in George's plane, I showed him the copy of the Metro News and pointed to Miti's story in it. He read it carefully while we sat in the cockpit of his aeroplane on the apron at Birmingham. Finally he looked up and said: "We must try to help this guy!"

George asked me to organize a trip to Britain for Miti, which he would pay for. After some phone calls, a travel agent was found (travel to and from Romania was still a bureaucratic quagmire, full of iron curtain suspicion and difficulty). Letters were passed between me and the British Embassy in Bucharest and a visa was arranged.

Finally on 22 February 1992, the Tarom flight from Bucharest with Miti on board landed at Manchester Airport. Karen and I were waiting to meet it. Miti was thrilled. It was the first time he had ever been outside Romania. He had finally arrived in the country whose language he had cherished for so many years.

Karen looked after Miti royally while he stayed with us. He spent a lot of time visiting businessman George and discussing with him the possibility of setting up a new business in Romania. He spent time also as a tourist and I actually got to see a lot of things in my country for the first time too. That's what it felt like to see them alongside Miti!

It soon became apparent that he was a star wherever he went. He had a way of speaking in a direct but polite way which endeared him to everyone. Also, because his English had been totally derived from BBC radio broadcasts, his accent had quite a 'posh' tang to it!

While he was with us he celebrated his 33rd birthday on March 6th. We had a slap up party at our house and invited just about everyone we could think of. Miti stayed with us until 21 April, when we took him to Gatwick to catch his plane back to Romania.

Romanian Rainbow: Miti and I watch a rainbow framing the giant Petro-Chemical plant at Navodari, near Constanta, summer 1992.

Gypsy convoy: On the road to Romania - our old charabanc and behind, two vans.

Above, in the home of Rudi and Helen (Miti's sister) at Navodari, July 1990. Left to right is Miti, Denise, Ramona, Rudi and Helen holding baby Claudia.
Below, in the same place eleven years later on 25 June 2001: Denise, Mandy, Helen, Claudia, Miti and Rudi pose for the camera.

Hands across a wall -
Outside Ceaucescu's massive Palace in the capital Bucharest, July 1990.

March 1992. Miti on his first visit to England, begins learning how to use a computer at my house in Birmingham.

August 1990, being baptised by assistant pastor Vic Nicolls (left) and Pastor Dave Woodfield.

Pastor Dave Woodfield recording one of the weekly 'Faith Walk' radio programmes at Grimm Doo, 1992.

TEN – METAMORPHOSIS

Vinnie

She always ran the water first thing in the morning – for a full five minutes. Then she would rinse and shake the contents of the kettle bone dry at least three times in an energetic jig before finally, it was ready to serve in the production of a cup of tea.

I witnessed this ritual everyday, or else heard its sacraments wafting in from the next room.

She was born in 1901, before an aircraft had flown, long before radio (or 'wireless,' as it was called) had appeared, when thoroughfares were called 'the horse road' because horses were the machines that travelled them and the motor car was a novel, odd rarity.

Vinnie – born 'Vinilia' in the year Queen Victoria died, was ten when the Titanic sank.

Of course I never called her 'Vinnie' – I called her mom! It was never the convention to call grown-ups by their first name, not until long after I was a grown-up too!

Mom came from another epoch. She inhabited a slice of time that was dressed in all the regalia of quaint etiquette along with a regimen of daily drudgery that has long vanished from this part of the planet. She ran the tap because in the Victorian slums of Birmingham where she grew up, you needed to clear all kinds of sediments from the pipe first thing in the morning.

Her speech was laced with those picturesque colloquialisms that abounded amongst the working class of the time:

"You'll laugh the other side of your face one of these days" she would say whenever I scoffed at her lofty pronouncements, which was often. I grew up a mocker in the shadow of those marvellous, self-exploding epithets which were once part of everyday day language, the standard currency of speech in the age she came from.

Vinnie had faith in abundance although she gave it away constantly. The more she gave away the more she had left. All sorts of people would come to her in need – for help, advice, or just the comfort of her ever-ready ear to their problems. She was a therapist to all who got to know her and the call of her counsel would draw to her doorstep the downtrodden and broken of all kinds: neighbours in trouble with the law, girls pregnant out of wedlock, drunkards, gamblers, homosexuals. She befriended them all, anybody in trouble. Vinnie would never be embarrassed at the things she would hear, although heaven knows, it was the other end of the universe from the place she inhabited. I think the only person who never came to her for advice was me!

Because of her beliefs, she constantly ran the gauntlet of her family. Their mockeries were exhibited if not verbally then in rolled eyes or else, hurtful indifferences toward her. But she was not to be swayed one iota.

"Only dead fish go with the tide" she would say (and there was never any doubt just where she thought the tide was heading for) "but it takes a live fish to swim against the current."

Buses

After dad died, it would often be just her and me out on some errand, visiting somewhere. In her gritty Victorian way, she showed me the bounds of her world, and I tagged along behind, a reluctant tourist. Proudly she would stand me at centre stage when she used to show my drawings of buses to aunts and uncles and the friends she met in Kunzles tearooms. *Isn't he clever? isn't he talented?* And in saying so, made it true for as long as the exhibition lasted. Pageants of scratchy paper, spread out on Formica-topped tea tables. They were like the first taste of the footlights to me; where I first became an addict for the approval of others. And how better to gain their approval than to draw buses? Giant ships that sailed from ports called bus stops to fanciful places I'd never heard of and longed to visit one day: Quinton Road West, Pheasey Estate, Lakey Lane Loop, wonderful enchanted places, surely better than Aston or Tile Cross, but maybe not quite as nice as Shirley, where mom's parent's lived.

Buses would take you wherever it was you desired to go – and in the fifties that meant with trimmed wood panelling and the smell of leather and cigarettes and a conductor who danced up the aisle with a ticket machine and a purse while up front, the driver sat in a cab sealed from the rest of us like some inscrutable warrior captain, responding to the coded bell signals from the conductor:

one 'ding' for stop, two for go, three for *go* and don't bother stopping at the next bus stop because we're full up!

Buses were to me, the most exciting and magical machines ever created, moving theatres of drama and promise. And to cap it all, dad had been a bus driver – yes, when I was born that was his job, and if I had anything to do with it, that is what I would be too, when I grew up!

Twilight

Then in December 1986 Vinnie fell down the stairs at Tile Cross and spent the night on the linoleum hall floor with a broken leg. Such was her stamina that she kept herself awake in the freezing cold, knowing that in the morning a postman would come and her only hope was to attract his attention. Somehow she made it through the night and in the morning the postman heard her cries and alerted the emergency services. Eventually a fireman broke the door down and by mid-morning Vinnie was safe and warm in East Birmingham hospital.

She never went back to live at Tile Cross after that, although for a long while she wanted to. One day while visiting the place with me she suddenly seemed to accept the inevitability of the new reality she was in and turned to me, declaring bluntly: "That's it David, I will never live here again. Sell it please!"

Joe had not been at Tile Cross the night of Vinnie's fall – he had been in hospital again with his 'nerves'. He was never able to look after himself and after her fall, Vinnie was no longer able to look after him, or herself, either. The result was they went into the care of residential homes and before too long, they were reunited at the same home in Selly Oak, Birmingham.

In September 1988, Joe went into hospital for the last time. Vinnie sat at his bedside all afternoon, just holding his hand until he passed away at eight fifteen in the evening. When I returned, she was sat alone in the corridor outside his room and I knew from her face he was gone.

Uncle Joe's funeral was the most amazing spectacle. Hundreds of people turned up, folk that he had touched with some kindness or else maybe one of his quintessent jokes usually attended with impromptu theatrics or music hall poetry. For Joe didn't just *play* a court jester, he *was* a court jester lost in the jokery for its own sake. He was oblivious to the titters and mocking graces of others.

Dave Woodfield gave a wonderful address quoting from Matthew: 'Well done, thou good and faithful servant'. The passage goes on to say 'You have been faithful with a few things; I will put you in charge of many things'. Joe had indeed been faithful with a few things. He was one of the meek and gentle of this world, powerless and un-ambitious, a lady's man who never married. I often wonder how he managed that.

There was a wonderful optimism in the air, the kind that often abounds at Christian funerals and brings you into that strange amphitheatre where grief and joy occupy the same space and neither is offended by the other.

The leg that Vinnie had broken falling down the stairs came back to haunt her in 1991 when a persistent ulcer turned into the creeping black of gangrene. When the dire situation was explained to us by the doctor at the hospital, she grabbed the forms and signed them resolutely, saying to me:

"David, it's going to kill me if I don't have it off. I want to live!"

She had her bad leg amputated and it made not one iota of difference to her outlook, even her mobility seemed only marginally impaired. She recovered in record time and was sitting up in bed exchanging jokes and small-talk with Karen and me on evening of the op.

We slowly became pals. Yes we did, and her gritty verdicts, always delivered with such Churchillian drama, became like anchors to me instead of the dead-weights they had been a lifetime before. We began to have fun and to laugh at the same things together. I was proud to be with her when we went out to a restaurant or on some jaunt to visit a friend or relative, and I know she was proud of me. I even began to take notice of her opinions and advice about things like love and marriage…

Divorce

By 1989, Karen and I had been together for 4 years. Pastor Dave suggested to me one day that we might want to get married. It hadn't occurred to me but as soon as Karen and I discussed it we both agreed it was the way forward. I checked with Pam in America that the divorce she had obtained in Reno was valid in the England and we made our plans and announced the date – 31 March 1989. Karen and I were married at the registrar office in Birmingham.

Vinnie was delighted. Karen and her got on well together and Karen was always a real good practical help to have around whenever we took Vinnie visiting.

We were married for four years and then something happened. A sad thing, in fact an unmitigated disaster:

One day at Christmas 1993, Karen left me. We had been growing apart for some time. In the beginning, she had dismissed my church experience but later had warmed to it. By 1993 the warming had long since cooled and was approaching absolute zero. Things got so bad between us that even the mention of the word 'church' stood a chance of causing an ugly scene. She had developed a yen for going out on the town with her friends and I had given up dissuading her, a fugitive from the arguments that might cause. Somewhere I thought it would be okay if we just hung in there but Karen was not a lady given to 'hanging in' anywhere and at some point she made the decision to leave. It was a shock. I descended into a period of intense self-examination, remorse and gloom.

Vinnie – yes it was about that time I started to call her 'Vinnie' – was tearful and terribly upset when I told her about it and as the days went to weeks, and weeks to months, the disaster of my second broken marriage had the effect of throwing us closer together. I found myself in need of her advice and she found herself in need of giving it. I became her patient; therapy sessions were held at any time, day or night, at the Lickey Hills Nursing Home, room number 20.

I was at my lowest point. I really bottomed out. I went to stay with Corky in America for a week in March, but just took my gloom with me. Back in England I joined a cookery class, went for counselling, worked on a new invention, wrote songs and answered the telephone with a sprightly 'hello' but it was just a vacuous façade and really I was desperately sad for a long time. Karen and I tried to recover our differences during our many meetings and phone conversations, but we never did. She would also pop in frequently on Vinnie (who she kept in close contact with) and I know Vinnie's heart for a long time was to broker reconciliation between us.

Early in 1995, after we had been apart over a year, Vinnie enumerated to me bluntly what the portends had already been screaming for some time:

"Karen's made up her mind, she's not coming back. You need to get on with your life David."

Commercial Pilot

I decided I would take a professional pilots licence course. It was something that had been bubbling away on the back burner for some time, aided by new regulations which said that to teach people to fly one must hold a commercial licence. I had been operating on what was generously called a 'Basic Commercial Licence' issued to instructors who had obtained their rating under the previous system as a 'grandfather right'.

And so in February 1995 I put my name down to begin a Professional Pilot's Licence course. It was a marathon of learning with several hurdles to jump: First there was six weeks of classroom tuition followed by exams. Then another course, more exams, and finally, extensive flying instruction followed by tests. The entire thing would cost the best part of £10,000 and take about eight months, and the odd thing was, I knew the Lord had prompted me to get on and do this.

Nevertheless I was full of doubts and excuses about it. "Who's going to look after my dog?" I said aloud to the wall at my empty house one day. Almost on cue, a short while later my friend Mark Jago called up:

"Dave, can I come and stay at your house please? I've got to get out of London. My girl friend's not my girl friend any longer and she's throwing me out of her house!"

So that was one problem solved. But then I thought of another: I didn't normally get up until mid morning! How on earth was I going to get myself to Coventry Airport and be bright eyed and bushy tailed by 8:30 every morning? I can't remember if I voiced that aloud but I remember thinking it before the telephone rang:

"Dave, it's Jon Poole."

"Hello Jon"

Jon ran the flying club at Birmingham Airport and I often used to instruct for him.

"Dave – I hear you've put your name down for the Commercial course at Coventry?"

"Yes that's right Jon."

"Well I'm on it too. But I've got a little problem: You know I've lost my driving licence don't you?"

"No I didn't know that Jon."

"Yes I have. And I was wondering, seeing as you and I are going to be doing this course together…"

"Yes?"

"I was wondering if er.., you could pick me on your way to Coventry. I'd pay your petrol money."

"Hmmm, not sure Jon. It's a bit out of the way. And I was just wondering how I was going to manage to get up every morning, I'd have to be up even earlier to pick you up!"

"Well there you go then" he said, "Problem solved! I'm up at 5 every morning, I can give you a wake up call if you can pick me up on your way."

That was it. Both my feeble excuses were answered. But I had a real good one for the encore. It was simply that I couldn't afford it!

"Don't Worry About the Money"

Those are the exact words I heard. They hit me like a sledgehammer and changed my outlook instantly. One second I was a winging naysayer and the next I was like a headstrong sweepstake winner. I felt as if I had just had a wad of money shoved in my pocket! I suppose it is *the substance of things hoped for, the evidence of things not seen* as the writer of Hebrews puts it.

One day I found myself driving along Bearwood High Street in my car and mulling it over in my mind I began worrying aloud about it and arguing with the Lord:

"This is crazy, I can't do it. There's no point me starting the course because I don't have enough money to complete it!"

I actually said it out loud and it was true! – I might have even added the words "So there!"

But the reply came like a firecracker through the letterbox on Guy Fawkes' night:

"DON'T WORRY ABOUT THE MONEY!"

It shut me up instantly. I felt a wave of peace rise up from deep inside like the caress of a warm hand and the money problem just evaporated completely out of my mind! It was so uncompromisingly definite, it just stopped me dead in my tracks. The fact was I had enough money to pay for the first part of the course (the six weeks of classroom tuition), so that's what I did. I began the course and discovered I actually enjoyed it. Well what happened, I hear you ask? Nothing at all for two months – Not until April 14, which happened to be both Good Friday and the last day of the course.

The postman had left a note in my letterbox the day before saying there was recorded delivery mail for me to pick up at the post office. It was an envelope from my publisher in Germany. I collected it and sped off to Coventry Airport without opening it, knowing it would be a few hundred quid of royalties from the hit 'Hiroshima' some five years previous. Anyway, I was late.

The weather man had predicted a gin clear day, I remember we had discussed it in the classroom the previous day, met forecasting being one of the subjects we studied. As I drove the twenty miles to Coventry Airport, a few wisps of low cloud thickened rapidly and turned the expected cloudless sunny day into a 'sea fret' – a continuous thin blanket of mist. Looking at the sky I was amazed but right then the Lord seemed to say to me 'I am in control'.

As it was the last day we were tying up loose ends, collecting sample question papers and other paraphernalia before leaving early. Around lunch time I reached in my bag and remembered the mail from the post office. I ripped it open and stared at the documents inside. I couldn't believe my eyes. There was enough money to pay for the whole course plus a bit! It was totally unexpected. I praised

God in my heart as I remembered that crazy promise: "don't worry about the money."

The cloud persisted most of that day, as if poking fun at the men at Her Majesty's Met Office, but I was riding high above it.

And that's not the end of it: At the end of April I spent two days in Leeds doing the exams and I have to admit that so many times, looking down at those papers, I felt 'helped' – that's the only way I can describe it – Now I don't want the CAA to disqualify me after the event for cheating, but the fact is the Spirit of God assisted me both with a clear mind and also with some prompting when the fog set in. The results came in mid May. I had sailed through everything. Out of the 15 students in our class at Coventry, I was the only one to take all nine subjects and pass everything! Others got through fewer subjects but none had passed all of them at one go. Yes I had powerful help. Please do not send a copy of this book to the CAA!

Gatwick

It was in late 1995 that I was undergoing a medical for the initial issue of a Commercial Pilot's Licence. For this I had to go down to the CAA headquarters at Gatwick Airport. The tests were very thorough and I spent several hours while nurses and doctors attached a whole panoply of apparatus to me and took readings. Finally a doctor ushered me into a consulting room.

There was just him and me.

"Sit down Mr.Morgan please. I just have a few questions to ask you and that will complete the examination."

"Okay" I said, relaxed that we were nearly done. I was sat at one end of a long room while the doctor was at the other end at his desk.

"Right" he said jumping to his feet. He grabbed a clipboard and began slowly striding back and forth along the length of the room. He seemed preoccupied with his clipboard and hardly glanced at me as he began asking questions while his pencil hovered above his pad.

"Has there ever been insanity in your family?"

"Yes"

He scribbled something on the pad.

"Have you ever contemplated suicide?"

I thought "Hang on a bit. There's no way they will let me fly an aeroplane if I answer yes to this!"

I swallowed hard…

"No" I lied.

He ticked a box on his pad barely seeming to notice me and carried on striding to and fro. Progressively moving down his list on the clipboard he finally came to this question:

"Is there any history of heart disease in your family?"

"Yes".

"Hmmm" he muttered and I saw his elbow move in a motion consistent with him etching a cross onto his pad.

"What was the relationship between you and the person that suffered from heart disease?"

"He was my father."

He stopped walking and looked up from his pad straight at me.

"He was your father?" he repeated back. I could see his expression had changed. That reassuring neutral smile was still there but his forehead now carried the makings of a frown.

"Yes" I confirmed.

"And what was the outcome?"

"He died"

His expression darkened like a scene from a Hammer film and a cold fog seemed to descend over the little consulting room. He frowned at his clipboard while a grunt of some kind came from his throat and I saw him scratch another cross on his pad.

"At what age did he die?" he asked. Now I could see I had his full attention plus a bit.

"Forty Two" I said.

If it's possible to gasp without making a sound, by just looking, that's what he did. His eyes widened in obvious shock and he stood transfixed for a few seconds staring down vacantly at his clipboard. – It probably said somewhere on it that I was already fifty three years old at this time.

Then with slow motion gravity he lifted his pencil and cleaved an emphatic cross onto his pad while the expression on his face darkened. Without a word he turned and strode to the far end of the room, sat down at his desk and began to shuffle though the papers lying there. He reached into my file and I saw him pull out the scroll of the ECG report I had just undergone. He unrolled it and began studying the squiggly lines closely, no doubt to search for the tell tale sign of faulty valves or blocked passageways that must have been missed by the cardiology nurse.

It was then; as I was watching him do this that the words came to me. I don't know where they bubbled up from. I think I've always had them whispering somewhere but then, at that moment, as I watched him scouring my records to find some reason to pronounce me sick, the words came and I shouted them in my thoughts as loud as I could, silently screaming at the doctor at the other end of the room:

I do not receive this message you are bringing. It does not belong to me and I do not receive it. The sickness that killed my dad is not mine, and I will not have it. It will have no part of me and I will not even think of it when I leave this room!

You have to understand I was not feeling any animosity to the doctor. It's was not his fault! He was doing his best to be helpful. He was thinking of the worst possible outcome. That's what he has to do, that's his job. But to stay alive and stay healthy I have to think of the best possible outcome. That's my job!

So I was refuting to myself the word of fear that he was bringing. I am quite sure that if I had accepted the statistical reality of my predisposition to congenital heart disease, I would have begun living in that reality. I would have altered my life style to accommodate the 'facts'. I would have begun operating in fear. And I believe fear itself is a risk to health as great as the thing I might be afraid of. Fear is like a cancer that eats into you and turns you into a piece of flotsam bobbing aimlessly on a sea of possible harm, sickness and death.

At the time I was on automatic pilot. It wasn't until some years later that I found just how important it is that when a word of fear comes against you, you have to counter it. Don't let it go unchallenged. That's my story anyway and I am sticking to it!

During most of 1995 I had busied myself taking the professional Pilot's Licence course while the legalities of becoming divorced went through their cold motions. Finally I completed the very last test of the pilot course and on the same day, a decree absolute was issued by the courts, ending my marriage to Karen. It was at the end of October 1995 when I paid her settlement fee and the flying tuition fees and was left flat broke!

April

Vinnie's sadness at Karen and me breaking up turned to the other extreme when I told her the news that Mandy and I were together in April 1996. A mother's happiness at the good fortune of her wayward son. She knew of Mandy as a Christian lady and she was over the moon to know I was with her and even more, when I told her that we planned to marry. One afternoon in her room she spoke to us both at length and gave a blessing over our union.

By now Vinnie was ninety-four years old and very frail. He once upright frame had shrivelled and shrunk so much that when she rode in my car she was unable to see the road ahead over the bonnet!

When I look back now, I can see that she relinquished something when she knew Mandy and I planned to marry. Like a weary warrior rests after a long battle ... She had lived her life for others, and I know she had lived for me over that period, until she knew I was okay. I don't really understand it but I know she had come to a place of completion, of resolution, and inside her worn out body, she was at peace. I saw it in her face.

One day at the end of May 1996, Mandy and I were discussing about getting engaged.

"I'm not very good at this. Have you ever bought a ring?"

"No."

"No, me either."

I had no idea what sort of ring to get. I had never been engaged before. Mandy left for Bradford where she still lived at the time, without us reaching a decision.

The next day after working as an instructor at Stratford, I drove up to see Vinnie in the evening. Her eyes were closed and her breathing very shallow. The faces of the nurses told me I should stay.

I sat holding her hand at her bedside, just like she had done with Joe. She opened her eyes just once and looked briefly at me. I saw a glimmer of recognition and a faint smile before she closed them again for the last time.

I called Mandy in Bradford to tell her. She had to work until midnight (waitressing at an Italian Restaurant) but insisted that she would drive down to be with me. Her car screeched to a halt outside my house in Birmingham at about two in the morning and we fell into a deep hug. Then we sat talking for ages and somewhere in the middle of it all, our attention fell upon a small brown envelope lying on the table. The nurse had pushed it into my hand as I left the nursing home earlier. On the outside she had hurriedly written: 'Vinnie's rings'.

I don't know who spoke first; it was one of those moments where words say an 'Amen' to what the spirit has already screamed... We both knew instantly that Vinnie's three gold rings should be the basis for our tokens of engagement and marriage.

Vinnie died on May 31st 1996, just six weeks after Mandy and I had come together.

She was a giant to me. A lady with a palpable, living faith. In the end, despite her disabilities or maybe because of them, I know that her example helped others not to lose heart when faced with life's challenges. And yes, this book is in part a celebration of her; I am not ashamed of that.

Vinnie's funeral, like Joe's before it, was an affair full of joy and hope, just as she would have wanted it to be. Dave Woodfield led the service and I sang a couple of songs at the church, standing right behind her coffin. I'd thought, "I wonder if I'll be able to do that?" – but whatever resources I didn't have the Lord provided. At the graveside committal, pastor Dave, always seeking to be the harbinger of lightness to the sombre situation, made an announcement of our intention to be married. We hadn't yet told Mandy's parents about it and as this incandescent newsflash was broadcast I saw Mandy's mom, Rose, sway visibly, to the point I thought she might fall down the hole right on top of Vinnie's coffin!

But Rose Scott, when we spoke afterwards, insisted that I was to call her 'mom' from then on. Which is what I do. I don't suppose she could appreciate exactly what that meant to me: I had become orphaned and gained another family, all in the space of a few weeks.

David Scott-Morgan

A month later in July, I changed my name by Statutory Declaration to David Scott-Morgan. Yes I wanted to make a declaration – a statement of God's audacious and bountiful goodness to me. I would have liked to engrave it on tablets and drape it on top of the Empire State, to make it as manifest in message as it was in fact. I had been rescued out of a slimy pit and scooped up to a high place. My horizon, once blighted by loneliness and divorce, had turned into a rich vista of amazing grace. God had brought me the most wonderful companion.

I am quite clear about it: I did not deserve Mandy.

Maybe I could have got a job with a famous group through my own efforts, and maybe I deserve to have my house, maybe I can pat myself on the back to have written a hit song and I dare say I can claim some worthiness for being able to fly an aeroplane, but I could NEVER have been married to Mandy without the Lord's help.

Mandy was, and is, my crown and the jewel in my crown. She is to me, the first prize, the jackpot, the garland, the bunting and the streamers all rolled into one! Her and me being together seems so natural now, but it wasn't that way to begin with. Quite the reverse.

Arranged Marriage

Yes I guess you could call it an arranged marriage. Mandy certainly didn't want it. Not at all. We were friends and that was as far as it went. Indeed she was severely offended by my approaches at first. But I had an odd sense of the inevitability about it all, like a premonition.

It was a strange and unfamiliar time for me. I was sailing on uncharted waters, suspended on a thread I didn't understand and responding to signals that were different from the carnal ones I was so used to. It was a new day for me in every way. New, deep, weighty and scary. I knew that the idea of Mandy and me being together was crazy, impossible and totally out of sync with reality. I was more then twenty years her senior, an old rock 'n' roller who had breezed into the church while she was a former missionary, a church worker who was waiting for the 'minister' she was to marry... But I had a vision. It had been planted so deep I couldn't dig it out!

And so we went through a period of circling around each other in some kind of Mexican stand-off but then finally, the day before her thirtieth birthday in April 1996, we got together. And that's the way it's been ever since.

Mandy has her own story of how that came about but essentially it's the same thing. She got a word from God that caused her to change her thinking. She allowed God to change her heart by testing out what He had suggested to her. A lot of people don't understand that the word 'repent' simply means to change your mind. That's all God ever asks us to do. He can do the rest!

God had said to Mandy in so many words: 'Why not Dave?' (those aren't the words, but they do express the thought). And Mandy had the courage to follow up on that.

It was an amazing time for me. Things were restored. Things that I had cast nonchalantly off and scorned in a former epoch – simple things that I had no right to expect to get back and surely didn't deserve. I learned to value marriage, courtship. Me, who had utterly scorned such things!

Mandy and I courted! We held hands and then after a while, we got engaged. I learned to do everything totally different to how I'd done for the thirty years before! Instead of going to bed first, we got married first!

Nowadays it's fashionable to talk about 'protected sex', but I had finally discovered what that really means – it's sex protected by God, because I do believe if you do it God's way, your protection becomes His business. Otherwise you're on your own! I knew all about doing things my way, and all about being on my own. Mandy was a virgin until we were married and I know now that the one place to have *protected sex* is under the covenant of marriage.

So I use the phrase 'arranged marriage' because that's just the way it seemed to me. It's my story and it's true. God arranged my marriage to Mandy and its one magnificent fact I will always thank Him for.

I underwent a metamorphosis. It took some time and it caused some pain. I shed some layers, some protections, some skins. I emerged a different person with a new pecking order of priorities and a new level of trust in God. It was a long night of despair before the dawn came, but when it finally came, boy what a sunrise that was! And all I can really tell you about it, all I have to share of any value is just this: God is good. Yes I went through a metamorphosis and coming out into the new day, I thought all the difficult stuff was behind me.

But I'd only just begun…

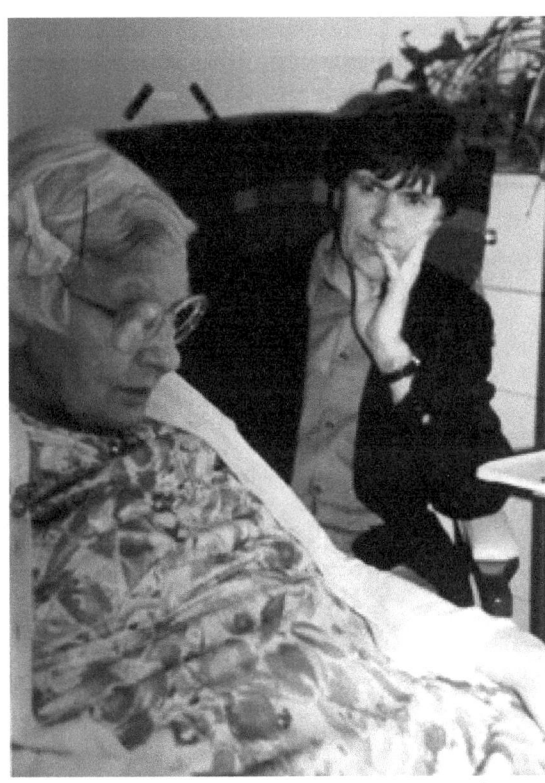

Vinnie 1994

Publicity shot of me and Mandy, 1998. (Foto by Paul Yates)

26 November 2000. Mandy and I play a rock n roll set at Ronnie Scott's, Birmingham, with the help of Tony Kelsey on guitar (above)

Playing at Bourton-on-the-water in the Cotswolds, 2000.

Airtax 964 Traffic Watch flight.
Staring in 1996, I fly about 200 early morning missions.

Flight instructing at South Warwickshire Flying School, Wellesbourne, near Stratford-upon-Avon. It's the club with the Vulcan bomber parked outside!

ELEVEN – HINDSIGHT

Part 1: Grimm Doo

I always thought I got my house because I was in an adulterous relationship with a lady; a lady who had happened to be walking past it one day, and noticed the 'For Sale' sign outside, and told me about it. That's how I thought the chain of events ran, but now I am not so sure it's that simple, although that part is that sordid.

We stood outside, me clutching the keys from the estate agent, while the 'For Sale' sign hovered in the front garden. Stepping inside we walked around its bare, dank rooms, me thinking it would be a love nest and she – well I don't know what she thought. She was silent and pensive, lost in some other empty place.

As soon as I walked inside I knew the house was for me. The front room looked as if it had been kitted out on purpose to be a recording studio: It had pegboard tiles on the ceiling in mock suggestion of sound-proofing and a small window set into an adjoining wall which gave the impression of looking into a control room instead of the living room. Later, many people thought that I had customised it like that but in fact it was just the way I found it.

Soon I had my recording equipment set up in the front room and was busy composing and recording music in my new home in Northfield.

But the lady who discovered the house? – she never came there again after that first day and our illegitimate love imploded on itself like a plutonium pit. Did I ever think the Lord could be somewhere in me getting that house with the shameful connection that led me to it? – No I definitely did not.

And yet…

It was December 1981 when ELO played at the NEC Arena in Birmingham. The NEC was the premier local venue and each of us in the group was allowed a block of complimentary tickets for our family and friends. Among my many guests at the four shows we did was Keith Sale and his wife Dorothy. Keith was the archetypal English gentleman, a man always brimming with a clean cut smile, a warm handshake, and sporting a walking stick that seemed to be of part sartorial and one part practical utility in aid of the slight limp he had from a knee injury.

It was just about one year before, at the end of 1980, that Keith had helped me obtain a mortgage for my new house. He had done this via a process of monetary magic that defied any logic I knew of: I was broke at the time and had no prospects of income. He didn't seem worried.

"Get your accountant to give me the last four years accounts" he said, "and I'll see what I can do."

It wasn't too long afterwards that he came on the phone to tell me he had secured a mortgage. I was amazed, how can you get a mortgage when you don't have an income?

Hindsight is great movie to watch. I can well recall that I had the house for about six months and then, just as the bills were mounting up, the job with ELO came up. From then on keeping the bills paid was no problem. Keith was to become a regular periodic visitor to my new home in Northfield, arranging insurances and dealing with all kinds of financial issues, which was his specialty.

I don't remember quite how it came about but at some point my home with its front room recording studio came to have the name 'Grimm Doo' attached to it. It was something to do with the fact the equipment was always a little less than optimum; For example, nothing was ever in stereo and that was grim for a start – according to Martin Smith. He was also convinced that the mixing desk growled at him whenever he went near it and so the name 'Grimm Doo' became enshrined into our impromptu folk lore, spelled with a double 'm' and a double 'o'.

I must have recorded over 200 songs on my 8-Track recorder and later, on a digital 16-Track at Grimm Doo. Richard Tandy, Martin and I spent many hours in that room slaving over hot recording machines and ELO even practised their stage set in there one day early in 1982.

Fast forward to April 1990 ...

It was nine years after buying Grimm Doo that I heard from a friend that Keith Sale had died suddenly. I went along to his funeral and was surprised at the difficulty I had parking my car. The church was laid back across an enormous expanse of grass verge that composed one side of Yardley Wood Road and there were cars parked everywhere. I was surprised again to walk inside the church and find it packed tight. People were squashed into every nook and cranny of the sanctuary and looking around at the faces gathered there I recognised several TV, music and sporting personalities.

Listening to the address I was amazed to discover that Keith had actually collapsed and died in that very church I was standing in, having worked there as a deacon for years. He had been a Christian all the time and I never knew it!

Fast forward another six years to 1996 ...

It was about six years later when I found myself with some time to kill in Birmingham City Centre one day and decided to call in at BCC, the big church where Dave Woodfield had been the pastor before. "Oh you must come and meet our new pastor" someone said. I shook hands with Brian Cole, and introduced myself.

"Hello" he said with a big warm smile as we walked along a corridor to his office.

"Dave Morgan?" he said knowingly, "that name rings a bell. Do you live in Halesowen?"

"No!"

"Do you ever go to Halesowen?"

"No!" I replied, and then added: "er well, I have gone there a couple of times. Only to pop in to my Building Society."

"Your building society?" he repeated.

"Er, yes."

"Hmmm,." he mused, "It wasn't the Britannia Building Society was it?"

"Yes it was!"

The quizzical furrow in his brow slowly resolved into a beam of recognition.

"Ah," he said, "Were you by any chance anything to do with Keith Sale?"

(!!)

We sat down in his office and he told me the story – how he had been the manager of the Britannia Building Society in Halesowen when Keith had come to him with my mortgage application. The reason why my name had stuck in his mind was that he had struggled with it for days:

"It sat on my desk, I really didn't know what to do about it. There was the question of income I recall. In the end, I don't know why, but I okay'd it."

Long Distance Serendipity

I was amazed at the slender line pulling together events over so many years. The two men who had been most instrumental in getting me my house were both Christians, and one was actually moved to do something against his better instincts on my behalf, all totally unknown to me. God had looked after me when I was a two-timing tearaway running as fast as I could the other way!

But it doesn't end there. Mom died in 1996 and was buried in Robin Hood Cemetery. I visited her grave one day and I was just walking away when the inscription on a nearby headstone caught my attention:

'Keith Sale' it said, and the name sang out like it was on a billboard in Times Square.

While writing this book I felt prompted to check it out further before writing about it (to make sure it was the same man and not another Keith Sale!). And so on Sunday 18th August 2002, Mandy and I went to the cemetery to check out the dates on Keith's headstone. As we walked up there was a lady tending a grave, Keith's grave. It was Dorothy, Keith's wife who I had last met twenty-one years ago at the NEC concert. She was visiting her husbands' grave that day because it was his birthday!

I told her the story of why we were there, of how Keith had helped me get my house all those years ago, how he had engaged the help of Brian Cole, how against the weight of wisdom the venture succeeded. She knew nothing of these details and was so happy to learn about it. The Lord blessed Mandy and me, and her, in that chance meeting.

I had stumbled across another strand in the web of God's Long Distance Serendipity…

Not a revelation of some life-changing mystery, but just a simple message, like the note a lover might leave under a pillow: 'I love you!'

What can you do but smile inside and wonder.

Grimm Doo was blessed with wonderful neighbours. John, Maisie and Pip, a theatrical family who used to present rumbustious comedy plays together (under the banner of 'Miss Mossie's Theatre Company'), owned the adjoining property. John and Maisie are gone now, but Pip, short for Phillip, inhabited the house next door to 'Grimm Doo' until 2005.

Yes now I see so many good things flowed from me being there in that house in Northfield, on the other side of town to where I grew up. And now I have to say like Jacob who was running for his life from the vengeance of the brother he had robbed and tricked, when he met with God: 'Surely God was in this situation and I was not aware of it'.

Part 2: Paper Round

Pop stars do not get up at five thirty in the morning. This is a fairly well documented fact.

If by any chance, a pop star *is* up at such an hour it is almost certainly because he or she hasn't gone to bed yet from the night before, or else maybe it's because like me, he isn't a pop star anymore.

Getting up early is one of those ordeals that the grown-ups would odiously recommend to me when I was a knee-high, held up shoulder high with a Rasputin stare and belching fumes into my pubescent face while thundering those cruel words: 'it's good for the soul'.

I was never that bothered to find out just how good it was for the soul. Not until an extra two and sixpence pocket money was dangled before me and I was goaded into taking a paper round. Yes, like many kids, I would grace the early morning streets and alleyways with my sack of papers, the clanks and squeaks of my bicycle being the only offence against the pristine silence of the new day.

Maybe that's where my aversion to getting up at the crack of dawn came from. Later on, my flirtation with pop stardom only served to reinforce my suspicion that no good thing happened before midday and getting up early was strictly for the birds.

Yes it was in 1996 I started doing another kind of paper round…

Jon Poole, who had been on the CPL course with me, told me there was a job going with his company at Birmingham Airport. (I was just beginning to think that all that training I had done the year before was a big waste of time).

"Let's go for a flight" Jon said "and I'll see how good you are!" Off we went for my first trip at the controls of his Seneca twin. I remember I did a perfect landing and he said "Fluke!"

I recoiled: "No it wasn't!"

But he was right, it was a fluke. The Seneca was not in the fullness of experience, an aircraft in which to do spot landings in. It was always a bit of an arrival.

But I was telling you about my paper round…

Well it wasn't *delivering* papers at all, but still in the business of feeding the hunger for news first thing in the morning. In my case the 'news' was that concerning the state of the road system around Birmingham.

- How heavy is the traffic?
- Is it moving or is it stuck?
- Are road works or accidents causing any hold-ups?

This was all accomplished from the elevated location of Jon's Seneca, which I flew while beside me, or else behind me with feet up, a radio presenter sat broadcasting information to the listening throng stuck in the world below. Usually it was a young lady who did that job, which seemed to require container-loads of ready wit as she exchanged small talk with the Disc Jockey managing the show from the radio station on the ground.

We would loiter like voyeurs swooping over the landscape, peeping down onto the tangled knots of motorised beings below. Orbiting over frozen junctions, espying a drip of traffic where there should be a torrent, our noisy presence announcing a freedom of action like a gloating boast, heaping further insult upon the grid-locked beings below. We would watch as spontaneous traffic jams appeared – especially on motorways – for no obvious reason, and then melted away again equally mysteriously. Traffic like a march of insects responding to invisible signals....

Yes this task, like the paper round, required me to arise at what is for me, a most disagreeable hour.

If that is indeed good for the soul – as the grown-ups used to claim – in the winter-time it must be a tonic finer than any water dispensed at Lourdes.

For three months in the winter, between November and February, I would take off before dawn, in what is known as the civil twilight (the pre-dawn halo). Actually a most un-civil time to be doing anything except sleeping. Striding out onto the tarmac with the tank of de-icing fluid strung over a shoulder, a broom in one hand, a torch in the other; a scarf, gloves and woolly hat to keep the hydraulics around the brain from freezing up. Yes it's positively therapeutic, you can feel the goodness coursing through you along with the icy wind....

On those early morning missions I would often bump into Ralph Hitchcock. He worked for the company that handled the corporate flights at Birmingham International Airport and it's a fact that him and me go back a long way: Years ago Ralph and I lived in the same road in Tile Cross and he was actually the manager of the first 'proper' group I was in – Jeff Silvas and the Four Strangers. And before that, we would often be hanging out as aircraft spotters together as we were both mad about aeroplanes, enough to swap reg numbers and photographs and visit air shows. Saturday morning bicycle expeditions would be arranged to Castle Bromwich aircraft dump where we would play inside the stacked fuselages of old Lancaster bombers, and steal mementos from them, before a watchman would come and shoo us away.

It's funny how our long-distance love for flying machines has induced us over the years to be in close proximity to them. I guess it's because deep down we are both still anorak aircraft spotters at heart.

Our traffic spotting flights from Birmingham used the callsign 'Airtax 964' – an honorific to the BRMB radio station and its frequency of 96.4. They would go everyday, regardless of weather and I would be rostered to fly it once or twice a week.

The only times that Airtax 964 was grounded was when the weather was threatening to go below our operating minima. Often it would be prudent to stay on the ground because the weather, being the most capricious of things, is able to frustrate the met men and their forecasts and leave Airtax Nine Six Four marooned up in the sky orbiting around waiting for unscheduled fogs to clear. We always carried enough fuel for such eventualities and in fact I never had to divert to another airport, but there was also the other problem that being a little aeroplane, it only had an outside toilet..!

I enjoy flying. I prefer doing battle with the elements rather than doing battle with people. The weather can be sneaky and duplicitous but it will not bear you a grudge and hunt you down if you beat it fair and square in combat. And the aeroplane will not say 'I don't ever want to see you again' if you lose your rag with it and tell it that it's useless in a moment of frustration.

Part 3: Songs, words and music

Songs come at night. Anyone who has ever messed with song-writing will agree with that. Even the ancients knew it[6]. Songs seem to manifest themselves at the most inconvenient times and the dead of night is definitely one of them. Often I have lay in bed with toes twitching to an imaginary beat and my head full of words and melody, thinking: 'shall I get up – or will I remember it tomorrow?' Because when a song comes, it comes with all the power of the now. You can't just ignore it.

If anyone is interested I will pass on a simple but effective rule that works for me. If a song is really that memorable – if it really is that good – you will remember it in the morning and in my experience it's safe to sleep on it. (But please don't write me an ugly letter if this doesn't work for you).

Now the song doesn't tell you that. The song is telling you how imminently precious it is and how if you don't get up and attend to its chords, or its riff, or its hook-line right away – it will leave you and go find somebody else who will treat it better. Don't panic! Songs are born as welfare junkies and spend their whole lives with dependency problems. They crave attention from the moment they burst out of the birth canal of your imagination into the world of men and plectrums. But I know well the fear that a writer can have of losing an idea – of not being able to remember something really special. Yes song-writing is a twenty four seven business if you love it like I do, you've got to give it everything plus a bit.

Words
"I want you to promise me you won't let your mother marry Alf!" granddad had said to me while he lay on his death bed in the upstairs room. I looked at the floor, scared to speak.

"Promise me!" he said again much louder.

I heard my choking voice squeak:

"I promise," and granddad, satisfied, lay back on his pillow and mumbled something about me being a good boy. He breathed a heavy sigh, his eyes staring straight above him. "I've had a good life" he said to the ceiling in a low voice.

And that was it. I had given my word to something I could not hope to do. I had promised something I had no way of accomplishing. I promised to influence mom to the point of changing her mind.

It caused me to secretly hope that words didn't mean anything. They were just something blown out of the lungs and lost on the wind. Because if words had any value or even worse, if there was any connection between future facts and words spoken in the now, then I was in trouble. Big time.

It's a terrible thing to discover that words *do* mean something when you are hoping that they don't; to find out that they hold power; that they are connected to what happens in the future.

Probably one of the only places where words really don't mean very much is in the ubiquitous three minute pop song. For sure I remember when I first began writing songs, musicians used to argue about it:

"Words are really, really important" said one.

"Nah rubbish. Nobody listens to the words, it's the tune that counts" said another.

People often ask me the question: which comes first – the music or the words? I have been asked this many times and given as many answers. It's just a perennial argument that rages to and fro and never settles into a place of rest. The egg comes before the chicken but the chicken has to lay the egg... Mmmm.

And then the other equally explosive question is:

'Which is more important – the music or the words?'

It's a fact that good music can catch your ear without you emphatically knowing what the lyric line is. You can test this from the many famous songs that have done quite well with an indifferent lyric line.

And yet it's a deeper truth that all really great songs have a great lyric too. I don't mean great poetry, where the words stand up on their own. I mean words that fit so well inside the musical frame that the two become one – music and lyric perfectly complement each other.

At the end of the day, a good song is where music and words get married and the one begets value from the other. Just as in life you get good marriages and bad marriages so in music you get good songs and the others...

I have written songs from both directions, words first or music first, but the best ones in my opinion are those where the melody comes with a snatch of words attached to it.

Music

I first got interested in music because of chords – especially the way chord changes sound – that great feeling you can get from one chord changing to another. I remember being at the Cinema as a kid and hearing the fanfare that introduced Twentieth Century Fox movies: I was so enthralled, it seemed like something that had come from another galaxy! It never crossed my mind that any man on earth could have made it up! It was just out of this world. Now I know a bit more about music and that it is the movement in the chords which really does it for me.

When I began to write songs, I quickly found out the building blocks of music is chords and that there is a relationship between them. That's right. Chords and melody were having an affair and me, and everyone else in the local Birmingham music scene wanted to know all about it!

In the sixties, the Beatles cannibalised the chord progressions of the previous generation and discovered new ones which sounded really exciting. Bass notes would climb or descend on the chord changes. The Beatles would delight in making one note stay the same while the chords changed behind it and that was a device that Jeff would later use with ELO productions. We loved all that kind of stuff and we would often chat about a new chord progression or technique we had discovered.

I remember for example, in the seventies, when I was playing the 'Rum Runner' residency with Magnum. One night Jeff came in and while we were on our break, he and I stood occupying a leaf of the bar, having a drink, and chewing the fat about songs. We got talking about the fact that a lot of pop music was based around identifiable chord structures. Somehow this discussion metamorphosed into playing a game where we both had to recognise the chords of whatever song was playing over the club's PA system. The rule was every time there was a chord change, the first one to bark out the new chord (and not have it challenged by the other), scored. "Let's say it's in the key of C" Jeff said, and the game began.

I remember that he was better at it than me and he won the game that night. But the point was that songs have structure, chord structure being one of them, and that was an ingredient of songwriting that we were all trying to understand and use.

When I look back on these events I realise how privileged I have been to have known Jeff Lynne over the years because he turned out to be a songwriter with a track record – somebody who actually delivered the goods. He proved he knew what he was talking about and I appreciate the understanding I have gleaned from being a spectator in the wings.

Later on when I was with Jeff in ELO I learned a lot from him about music. One thing I noticed was how he had taken the trouble to think through a lot of things that I had simply passed by or ignored. For example when we were recording, he once asked me to sing with a sharp edge to my voice and I said "why don't you do that sound on the desk with EQ" (equalisation). He replied that "you can do it there too, but you can also change the sound of your voice by the way you sing!" As soon as he said it, I realised I already knew it and had used that technique myself, but somehow I'd never thought it was the 'proper' way to do it. My first response was change it using the recording machinery on the desk but he had thought it through and would do both. It was a sobering thought for me. He had taken the trouble to study it carefully. That was one difference between us. I hadn't.

I remember that Jeff would never let anyone contribute words or melody to his songs. I don't think it was fear of litigation, I think it had to do with the pride he took in his work. One time I saw him trying to get a line for a song in the studio[7] and I proffered something as a possibility, but immediately he shot back with: "No, don't help me!" and disappeared with head down, back into scribbling-on-pad mode. A little later he explained to me : "Don't say anything Dave because if you come up with something really good I'll be sick that I won't be able to use it."

I was never so conscientious myself. One time I remember Jeff wrote some words to one of my songs when I was stuck but he flatly refused to be credited for it!

And now, how very strange it is to see that solid things made of concrete, stone and steel have disappeared without a trace. Things like buildings and streets have gone forever and yet the songs that inhabited them still remain long after the bricks and mortar are smashed to dust. And so places like Penny Lane and Strawberry Fields will exist in the vapour of music when their namesakes lie beneath motorways or theme parks.

What a strange, powerful thing this music is. What magic, what exotic potion to wield such strength and yet look so feeble. Unassuming, like a warrior wearing the coat of a fool. What a privilege to work it and wield it.

Epilogue

I have to fill in a form in order to hire a car. What a trauma, I hate it. The question looms what *is your job?* And straight away I am in a panic:

What is my job?

Shall I put *drifter and opportunist?*

Maybe I should put *writer* or *pilot* for I do write songs and I do fly planes. But somehow that seems fraught with problems – for sure the next question will be "What hit song did you write, maybe I know it?" or "Which airline do you fly for – I went to Ibiza on Monarch, maybe you were driving?"

Maybe I should put *musician*, well that's certainly true (but will they still let me have their car?) Maybe *pastor* – although that implies an income, which is not the case. After all, the word 'job' is descriptive of something that renders money.

So I am forever wondering who I am.

"Can we leave that blank please?"

"Oh, so you are unemployed huh?"

"No, I am employed up to my eyeballs in tasks day and night actually. But...."

So you must edit my thoughts in the light of the fact my box marked *who are you?* is completely blank.

Who am I and what do I do?

I look out for signals coming in, patterns in the chaos.... and if I should say boldly that I believe God is doing this or that now, it is only because I am quite clear that God has already done this or that then, before, previously.

The 'In the beginning God' set something going, and unlike me, He does not abandon his plans in midstream, or get distracted....

Science calls it 'synchronicity' – meaningful related events, but that antiseptic word is but a smear of toothpaste to freshen the mouth of those who have never tasted the substance of synchronicity in their gut, and never known it's directed elegance in their life, for if they had, they would tack on the word 'divine' somewhere. It has to be divine synchronicity, for without that, the 'meaningful related event' is in fact a *meaningless* related event!

So many things have happened to me that fall into the category of a meaningful related event, that I grow tired of the word 'coincidence'. Still, I know how dear that word is in the chaotic world of chance that science has bequeathed us, so I use it in order to communicate with the outside world, to explain. And anyway it's a lot shorter than *divine synchronicity*.

In the end, the patterns in the chaos – the evidence of divine synchronicity – can only be discerned, if at all, from the perspective of time, like a fog from afar becomes a cloud. Time is the one thing the eternal God has plenty of, the one thing of which we have very little. But if He grants you enough of it, and you look carefully, I'm sure you will find some of those patterns for yourself.

Discography 1: Dave's Record releases

	Year	Name	Artist etc
	1970	**MORGAN LP** ~~AMPEX A-10118~~	Morgan 11 tracks
	1978	**MORGAN-CLEARY LP** ~~Jet Records~~	Morgan-Cleary 10 tracks 5 songs by DM, 5 by Jim Cleary
	1979	**One More Day 7"** Evolution Records EV3	Morgan 2 tracks B side = 'Princeton'
	1983	**EARTH RISE LP** Parastar WKFM LP 68 LP	Tandy-Morgan 13 tracks
	1984	**Berlin 7" & 12" EP** Sonet records SON2274	R&D (Richard & Dave) 3 tracks B side 'This is the Day'
	1988	**Action 7" & 12" EP** FM Revolver UK FM VHF 26	Tandy Morgan Band 4 tracks
	1990	**ALL GOD'S BLESSINGS Cass** ~~Dave Scott-Morgan AGB~~	Dave Morgan 17 tracks various compilations
	1991	**Bethlehem Town 7" + Cass** ~~Sovereign Records SOV107~~	Dave Morgan 2 tracks B side Christmas Bells
✓	1992	**EARTH RISE CD** Prestige Records CDSGP015	Tandy-Morgan 12 tracks Also on Cass
✓	1992	**B.C. Collection CD** Dave Scott-Morgan TMS92	Tandy Morgan Smith 17 tracks + 1 dummy track – ('Traction')
✓	1997	**CALL CD** Dave Scott-Morgan CDM97	Dave Scott-Morgan 16 tracks
✓	1999	**Long Way Home CD** Dave Scott-Morgan LWH	Dave Scott-Morgan 12 tracks
✓	2001	**REEL TWO CD** Dave Scott-Morgan R201	Dave Scott-Morgan 16 tracks 2 by JimCleary, 1 Beatles
	2002	**ANGEL LIGHT CD** Luis Miguel LMA1	Dave Scott-Morgan 10 tracks
	2002	**PROJECT FREEDOM CD** ~~ELO Fan Club Holland~~	Dave Scott-Morgan 3 tracks
	2004	**The Complete UGLY'S CD** ~~Sanctuary CMQCD919~~	The Ugly's 23 tracks 5 tracks written by DM
✓	2011	**EARTHRISE Special Edition CD** Rock Legacy ROL2011	Morgan Tandy 15 tracks
✓	2012	**ACROSS THE DIVIDE CD** Grimm Doo Records GDR2012	Morgan 11 tracks
↓	2014	**All True Love** single Digital BarCode 888174630366	Dave Scott-Morgan
↓	2014	**21 Today** single Digital BarCode 859713457782	Four Twenty One DM + Phil Hatton

✓   Available from www.davescottmorgan.com

↓   Download from iTunes, Amazon etc.

Discography 2: Other releases / other artists

Year	Title / Label		
1966	Now that I love you so 7"	Two's Company	
	Polydor BM56072	DM + John Fincham	
1969	I've seen the Light 7"	The Ugly's	
	~~MGM 1465~~	b/w Mary Colinto	
1968	Private Airman Harris	Ian Campbell Folk Group	
	Essex	Re-titled 'Private Harold Harris' (!)	
1969	Something	The Move	
		B side of 'Blackberry Way'	
1970	This Time Tomorrow	The Move	
		B side of 'Curly'	
1969	**PARADOX** single	Paradox (Bob Catley)	
	Mercury	Eversince I can Remember / Mary Goodbye	
1970	**WISHFUL THINKING** Album	Wishful Thinking	
	Global 6306 903	12 tracks incl. Hiroshima	
1975	**Baby I Need**	Magnum	
	~~CBS2959~~	B side: Moving On by Tony Clarkin	
1985	**Nineteen Eighty Five**	Shawn Moran	
		B side of 'Motor Bikin' Produced by R&D	
1986	**Action** LP	Various Artistes	
	FM TED1	Includes Action instrumental	
1987	**Distortions** FILM	Dave Morgan	
		9 specially written tracks.	
1991	**Hiroshima**	Sandra	
	Virgin 663015 CD	European Hit Produced by Michael Cretu	
1999	**Friends & Relatives** CD	Various Artistes	
	Eagle EAG 176-2	Incl '3 tracks from Tandy-Morgan EarthRise	
2006	**Brumbeat** CD	Various Artistes	
	Castle CMEDD 1146	Incl 'Mary Colinto' by Paradox	

(crossed out = not released or no longer available)

Also available from Lifeware Publishing:

I Will Rise and Stand
by Sandie George

Sandie George's roller coaster life story is a book to warm the cockles of your heart.
This epic story leaves you feeling all kinds of things: hope, peace, thankfulness. A tour de force, a cliff hanger and a breath of fresh air all at once.

With Apologies to Solomon
by David Scott-Morgan

A collection of tongue-in-cheek homilies, each one coupled with a humorous cartoon drawn by Dave.

www.LifewarePublishing.com

Footnotes:
[1] The Rockin Berries: 'He's In Town' b/w 'Flashback' - reached number 3 in May 1964.
[2] Jefferson: 'I love you this much' - Philips 6308 166 1973.
[3] Richard Tandy & Dave Morgan: 'Earth Rise' recorded after ELOs TIME tour in the early 80s.
[4] In 1994 Frank Skarth-Haley drowned while sailing a fishing boat at night off the north coast of France.
[5] My version of Jim Cleary's song 'Modeste the Minor Poet' was released on the Reel 2 CD in 2001.
[6] Psalms chapter 42 verse 8: By day the LORD directs his love, at night his song is with me...
[7] Wissellord studios, Hilversum, Holland, 1982. Working on the album 'Secret Messages'.

L - #0119 - 211019 - C0 - 210/148/12 - PB - DID2653401